Table of Contents

Chapter 1: Industry Overview
For Those Interested in the Insurance Industry 2
Insurance: Financial Protection From Risks 3
By the Numbers 3
How Insurers Make Money 4
The Economics of Insurance 5
How Insurance Is Sold 9
Important Functions of Insurance Organizations 11
Insurance Entities 13

Chapter 2: Property/Casualty
Property/Casualty Market at a Glance 20
Property/Casualty Coverage Types and Lines of Business ... 22

Chapter 3: Life & Annuity
Life Market at a Glance 34
Life Insurers Chasing Wider Range of Opportunities 36
Important Lines of Life Business and Products 38
Annuity Products 39
Accident & Health Products 41

Chapter 4: Health
Health Market at a Glance 49
Developing Issues for Health Insurers 50
Major Types of Health Plans 52
Products and Terms 52
Common Health Insurance Terms 53

Chapter 5: Reinsurance/Alternative Risk Transfer
Overview of Reinsurance 59
Developing Issues in Reinsurance 61
Alternative Risk Transfer and Risk Financing 62
Insurance-Linked Securities and Structured Transactions .. 62

Chapter 6: Fiscal Fitness & AM Best
Insurance Stands Traditional Product Cycle on Its Head ... 73
The Risk of Financial Impairment 74
Overview: Best's Credit Rating Evaluation 75
AM Best's Insurance Information Products and Services 77

Spotlights
Does Insurance Cause Some People to Lie? Behavioral Economics Has the Remedy 15
Survey: Colleges Need to Better Prepare Future Insurers for Real World 17
Automakers Build New Insurance Future 27
Insurance Coverage Questions Surround Emerging NIL Industry 32
Staid Annuities Get Star Treatment in Movie About the Importance of Guaranteed Retirement Income 42
Startup Founder Hopes to Help People Find 'Ferrari in the Garage' by Taking Life Settlements Mainstream 45
Biometrics Laws and Regulations Poised to Become a Flashpoint for Insurers, Market Watchers Say 54
Legalized Recreational Marijuana Is a Growing Business With Insurance Challenges 56
FIU Extreme Events Director: Prototype Facility Will Test Forces of a Cat 6 Hurricane 66
Insurance Leaders: Time to Better Protect, Shore Up Coastal Homeowners' Properties 71
COVID-19 Mortality Trends, Interest Rates and Climate Change Seen as Key 81

Best's Guide to Understanding the Insurance Industry

2023 Edition

Published by AM Best

AM BEST COMPANY, INC.

OLDWICK, NJ

CHAIRMAN, PRESIDENT & CEO: Arthur Snyder III

SENIOR VICE PRESIDENTS: Alessandra L. Czarnecki, Thomas J. Plummer

GROUP VICE PRESIDENT: Lee McDonald

AM BEST RATING SERVICES, INC.

OLDWICK, NJ

PRESIDENT & CEO: Matthew C. Mosher

EXECUTIVE VICE PRESIDENT & COO: James Gillard

EXECUTIVE VICE PRESIDENT & CSO: Andrea Keenan

SENIOR MANAGING DIRECTORS: Edward H. Easop, Stefan W. Holzberger, James F. Snee

DESIGN & PRODUCTION

SENIOR MANAGER: Susan L. Browne

DESIGN/GRAPHICS: Jenica Thomas, Angel M. Negrón

ISBN: 9798386084738

Copyright © 2023 A.M. Best Company, Inc. and/or its affiliates. ALL RIGHTS RESERVED. No portion of this content may be reproduced, distributed or stored in a database or retrieval system, or transmitted in any form or by any means without the prior written permission of AM Best. While the content was obtained from sources believed to be reliable, its accuracy is not guaranteed. For additional details, refer to our Terms of Use available at AM Best website: www.ambest.com/terms. Articles from outside contributors do not necessarily reflect the opinions of AM Best.

For Those Interested in the Insurance Industry

AM Best publishes *Understanding the Insurance Industry* to provide a clear picture of how the insurance industry operates, generates revenue and provides opportunities for people of varied talents and interests.

It's designed to provide readers with a high-level overview of the insurance industry, particularly how it operates in the United States. It's also designed to be a gentle and broad introduction to the insurance industry for students, new employees, prospects and those who would like to learn more about one of the most interesting and important financial services industries.

We've designed this book in six sections: industry overview, property/casualty (also known as nonlife insurance), life, health, reinsurance and alternative risk transfer, and the function of AM Best in the industry.

Articles were prepared by members of AM Best's editorial team. Some content is extracted from *Special Reports* produced by AM Best, from articles in *Best's Review* magazine and from reporting specifically for this edition.

Order Additional Copies

More Information and Resources

Chapter 1: Industry Overview

Insurance: Financial Protection From Risks

Insurance protects against the financial risks that are present at all stages of people's lives and businesses. Insurers protect against loss—of a car, a house, even a life—and pay the policyholder or designee a benefit in the event of that loss. Those who suffer the loss present a claim and request payment under the insurance coverage terms, which are outlined in an insurance policy. Insurers typically cannot replace the item lost but can provide financial compensation to address the economic hardship caused by a loss.

All aspects of life include exposure to risk. Individuals and businesses are presented with the following choices: Accept the risk and the consequences of a loss if it happens, avoid the risk by not engaging in the risk-taking activity, or manage the risk by procuring insurance. Those who don't procure insurance coverage are responsible for the full loss. Those who obtain coverage succeed in "transferring the risk" to another organization, typically an insurance company.

Purchasing insurance is the most common risk transfer mechanism for people and organizations. The money paid from the insured is known as the premium. In return, the insurer agrees to pay a designated benefit in the event of the agreed-upon loss.

By the Numbers

Insurance takes advantage of concepts known as risk pooling and the law of large numbers. Many policyholders pay a relatively small amount in premiums to protect themselves against a possible larger loss. When a sufficient number of insureds make that same choice, the funds available to pay claims

www.ambest.com

Chapter 1: Industry Overview

increase, and the chances of any single person or group exhausting the available funds grow smaller.

In risk pooling, insurers can accept a diverse and large number of risks, so long as many people participate in the insurance process, and the insured risks are individually unpredictable and infrequent. Although an insurer may accept risks from a large number of people, only a small portion of those are likely to suffer an insured financial loss during the period of insurance coverage. Risk pooling allows insurers to pay claims to the few from the funds of the many.

What insurers sell is protection against economic loss. These losses are outlined in contracts or documents known as insurance policies.

Life and health insurers cover three general areas:
- Protection against death.
- Protection against poor health or unexpected medical costs.
- Protection against outliving one's financial resources.

Nonlife insurers, known as the property/casualty sector in the United States and Canada, in general offer two basic forms of coverage:
- Property insurance provides protection against most risks to tangible property occurring as the result of prespecified perils such as collision, fire, flood, earthquake, theft or other perils.
- Casualty, or liability, insurance is broader than property and often provides coverage of an individual or organization for negligent acts or omissions.

A well-known form of casualty insurance, auto liability coverage, protects drivers in the event they are found to be at fault in an accident.

A driver found to be at fault may be responsible for medical expenses, repairs and restitution to other people involved in the incident.

How Insurers Make Money

Insurance companies primarily make money in two ways: from investments and by generating an underwriting profit—that is, collecting premiums that exceed insured losses and related expenses.

It all begins with underwriting. Insurers, whether life or nonlife, must assess the risk and gauge the likelihood of claims and the value of those claims.

Insurance companies invest assets that are set aside to pay claims brought by policyholders. The insurance "float" represents the available reserve, or the funds available for investment once the insurer has collected premiums but is not yet obligated to pay out in claims.

If an insurer has predominantly short-term obligations—for example, homeowners' policies which pay out in a relatively short period— the float is usually invested in short-term liquid instruments to enable the insurers to pay out on claims as they happen.

If the needs are long term, a portfolio containing fixed-income securities, such as bonds and mortgage loans, may also include preferred and common stocks, real estate and a variety of alternative asset classes.

Life insurers also establish separate accounts for nonguaranteed insurance products, such as variable life

Chapter 1: Industry Overview

insurance or annuities, which provide for investment decisions by policyholders.

Property/casualty insurers traditionally have been more conservative with the asset side of their balance sheets, primarily due to the high levels of risk on the liability side. For example, catastrophe losses can wipe out years of accumulated premiums in some lines.

The global recession of the previous decade hurt nearly all aspects of the insurance industry, as many companies experienced declining revenues and investment losses. Companies with risky asset portfolios such as an outsized exposure to mortgage-backed securities, equities and high yield bonds suffered disproportinately.

Life insurers who offered variable annuity products with rich guarantees to their policyholders also suffered, as they used options to hedge these guarantees. During a time of peak stock market volatility, these options became very expensive, resulting in losses.

Few winners emerged. However, the mutual insurance sector managed to remain somewhat unscathed by the downturn. Ater the recession, meanwhile, the Federal Reserve's attempts to battle the economic weakness by lowering the fed funds rate resulted in a chronic low interest rate environment limited the ability of life and other insurers to benefit from fixed investments such as bonds. That may change, depending on economic conditions that could spur higher inflation.

The Economics of Insurance

More than 2,624 property/casualty companies and 742 life/health insurance companies are included in AM Best's files for the United States and Canada. AM Best's global database includes information on more than 17,000 insurance companies worldwide. Insurers pay claims in property, liability, life, health, annuity, reinsurance and other forms of coverage. In the United States alone, the broader insurance industry provides employment to 2.8 million people.

Insurance organizations play a vital role in the U.S. and other economies. They protect individuals and businesses from unexpected financial loss. Money they receive as premiums is invested in the economy. Protection from financial loss provides a sense of security to individuals and businesses, which are freer to pursue business and personal opportunities with less worry about financial devastation. Businesses can afford to purchase real estate and equipment, to hire more employees and fund expansion.

Premiums collected from insureds, often known as policyholders, are invested by insurance organizations

US Insurance Industry – Jobs by Sector

U.S. Insurance Employment	2.84 million
Insurance Agencies and Brokerages	913,200
Direct Life and Health Carriers	909,300
Third-Party Administrators	211,200
Claims Adjusting	55,600
Direct Title and Other Direct	95,100
Direct Property/Casualty	532,000
Reinsurance Carriers	26,200

Source: U.S. Department of Labor.

Chapter 1: Industry Overview

Insurance Density – Annual Per Capita Insurance Premiums (2020)

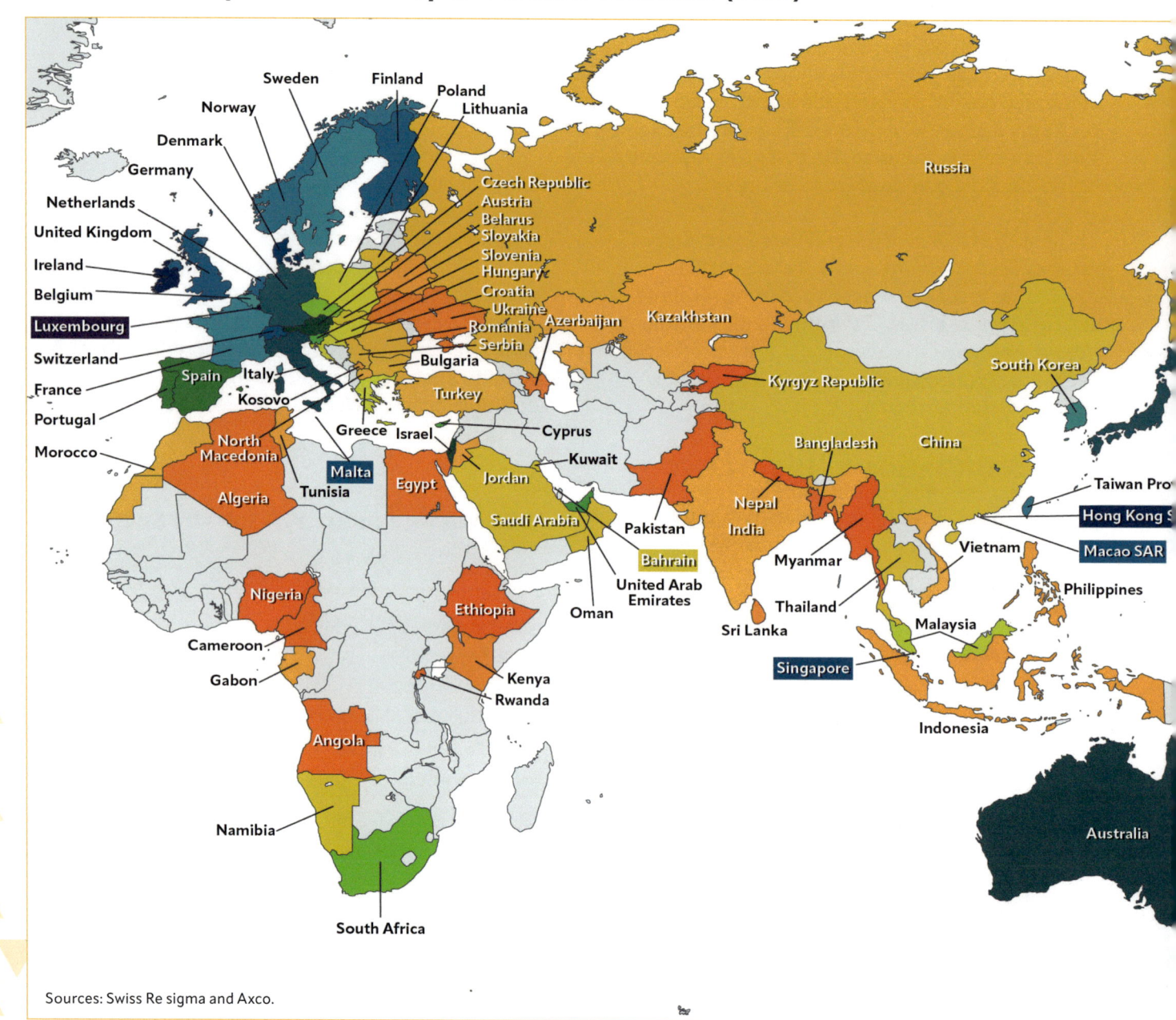

Sources: Swiss Re sigma and Axco.

Chapter 1: Industry Overview

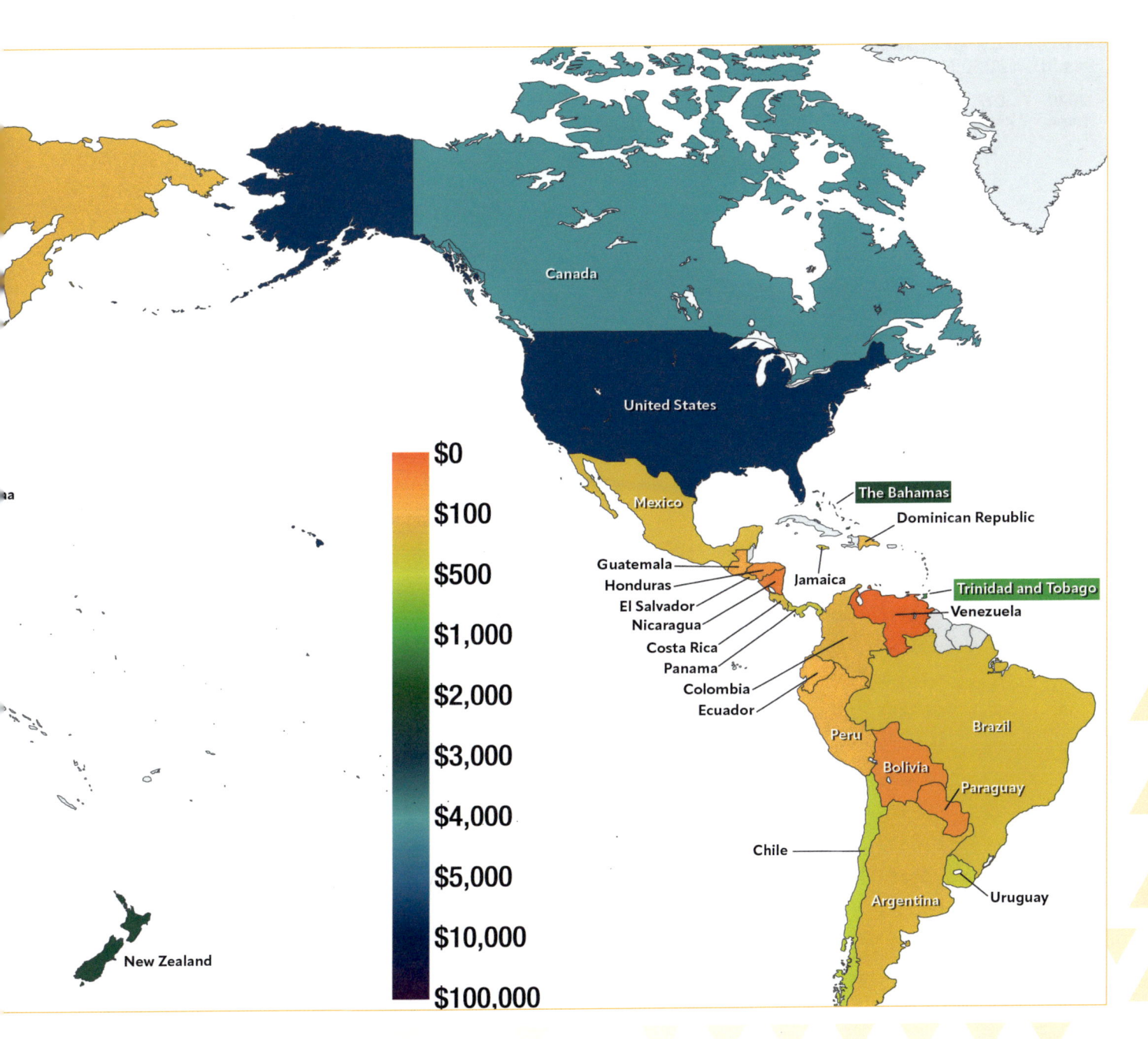

Chapter 1: Industry Overview

Best's Rankings
World's Largest Insurance Companies – 2023 Edition
Based on 2020 Net Nonbanking Assets.

2020 Rank	2019 Rank	AMB#	Company Name	Country of Domicile	2020 Net Nonbanking Assets (US$ 000)	% Change*
1	1	085014	Allianz SE	Germany	1,261,940,234	4.90
2	3	085085	AXA S.A.	France	950,598,568	2.77
3	2	058182	Prudential Financial, Inc.	United States	940,722,000	4.93
4	8	086446	Ping An Ins (Group) Co of China Ltd	China	883,921,884	16.49
5	4	058334	Berkshire Hathaway Inc.	United States	873,729,000	6.85
6	6	058175	MetLife, Inc.	United States	795,146,000	7.38
7	5	090826	Nippon Life Insurance Company	Japan	776,720,328	6.88
8	10	052446	China Life Insurance (Group) Company	China	776,376,157	12.15
9	7	086120	Legal & General Group Plc	United Kingdom	774,781,625	1.75
10	11	066866	Manulife Financial Corporation	Canada	688,785,058	8.80
11	13	085124	Assicurazioni Generali S.p.A.	Italy	669,121,764	5.86
12	12	085909	Aviva plc	United Kingdom	651,607,417	4.31
13	9	095689	Japan Post Insurance Co., Ltd.	Japan	636,812,794	-2.08
14	16	058702	American International Group, Inc.	United States	586,481,000	11.70
15	14	046417	Dai-ichi Life Holdings, Inc.	Japan	577,106,514	5.97
16	17	085244	Aegon N.V.	Netherlands	546,475,851	0.98
17	18	086056	CNP Assurances	France	543,616,259	0.49
18	19	093310	Crédit Agricole Assurances	France	536,783,775	2.71
19	15	090906	National Mut Ins Fed Agricultural Coop	Japan	531,654,523	1.47
20	21	085485	Life Insurance Corporation of India	India	520,495,238	18.99
21	20	085925	Prudential plc	United Kingdom	516,097,000	13.62
22	26	050910	Great-West Lifeco Inc.	Canada	469,823,376	33.10
23	22	050457	Zurich Insurance Group Ltd	Switzerland	439,299,000	8.55
24	23	090828	Meiji Yasuda Life Insurance Company	Japan	417,243,955	7.89
25	24	061691	New York Life Insurance Company	United States	414,250,000	11.46

* Percent change is based upon local currency.
Source: *Best's Financial Suite-Global*; data as of Dec. 13, 2021.

Chapter 1: Industry Overview

until they are paid out. Investor Warren Buffett has famously championed the value of "float"—funds held by insurance companies until they must be paid—as an important source of investment capital. However, insurers must be cautious and risk averse with the majority of their investments, both to satisfy regulators' demands and to be able to pay unexpected and large claims.

Insurance companies are large holders of bonds, particularly those issued by corporations and similar sources. They typically invest small portions of their available funds in stocks. Life insurers have traditionally played larger roles in real estate investments, although a portion of those investments has shifted from direct ownership of commercial properties to more liquid investments in real estate investment trusts and the like. Insurers have also funded mortgages for commercial borrowers and developers, which in turn use the money to build commercial centers, shopping centers, apartments, warehouses and houses.

The insurance industry is part of the larger financial services industry, which includes banks, brokerages, mutual funds, credit unions, trust companies, pension funds and similar organizations. Traditional barriers between industries have disappeared in part. Mutual funds can be sold by insurance companies and banks. Equities brokers handle cash management accounts. Banks have become active sellers of life insurance and annuities and other insurance products. Insurers themselves have developed products that include savings, protection and investment elements.

How Insurance Is Sold

Insurance is sold through a variety of channels, including face to face by insurance agents and brokers, over the internet, through the mail, by phone, in workplace programs and through associations and affinity groups.

Insurance agents can be exclusive—tied to a particular insurer—or independent, representing several insurers. Insurance brokers usually represent the insured client but can sometimes act as an insurance agent.

The insurance agent (or producer) can be a key component in the underwriting process by taking the role of intermediary.

Unlike the underwriter, the agent is positioned to meet with the applicant, ask pertinent questions and gauge responses. Information gathered from the interview may become the basis the underwriter uses in decision-making. As a benefit to the consumer, many agents—called independent agents—represent several insurance companies, and may have a better view of each company's risk-selection threshold.

A "captive" or "tied" agent works primarily with a single insurer or a group of insurers, and may receive business leads or some sort of special preference for having that relationship. The insurer often offers benefits, such as health coverage, marketing support and training to the captive agent.

Generally speaking, insurance companies with a captive agent force also may see better policyholder retention. For starters, independent agents are less likely to follow policyholders from one state to

www.ambest.com

Chapter 1: Industry Overview

Best's Rankings
World's Largest Insurance Companies – 2023 Edition
Based on 2020 Net Premiums Written.

2020 Rank	2019 Rank	AMB#	Company Name	Country of Domicile	2020 Net Premiums Written (US$ 000)	% Change*
1	1	058106	UnitedHealth Group Incorporated [1]	United States	201,478,000	6.21
2	2	086446	Ping An Ins (Group) Co of China Ltd	China	118,754,056	0.14
3	4	052446	China Life Insurance (Group) Company	China	111,156,155	6.20
4	10	051149	Centene Corporation [1]	United States	107,370,000	49.72
5	6	058180	Anthem, Inc.	United States	105,726,000	11.61
6	5	070936	Kaiser Foundation Group of Health Plans [2]	United States	102,933,365	5.85
7	3	085085	AXA S.A.	France	101,308,605	-8.68
8	7	085014	Allianz SE	Germany	93,645,846	-1.47
9	8	085320	People's Ins Co (Group) of China Ltd	China	79,573,492	-0.14
10	9	085124	Assicurazioni Generali S.p.A.	Italy	79,193,720	-2.74
11	12	058052	Humana Inc. [1]	United States	74,186,000	17.85
12	11	020013	State Farm Group [2]	United States	71,116,271	0.19
13	13	058334	Berkshire Hathaway Inc.	United States	64,901,000	3.33
14	14	086577	Munich Reinsurance Company	Germany	64,294,456	7.24
15	16	070080	CVS Health Corp Group	United States	56,701,017	8.99
16	17	085485	Life Insurance Corporation of India	India	55,008,395	6.27
17	18	090598	China Pacific Insurance (Group) Co Ltd	China	51,701,496	3.74
18	15	090826	Nippon Life Insurance Company	Japan	46,283,351	-9.22
19	25	069154	Health Care Service Corporation Group	United States	44,910,745	12.13
20	21	090906	National Mut Ins Fed Agricultural Coop	Japan	44,140,813	5.95
21	29	085068	HDI V.a.G.	Germany	43,481,675	3.87
22	19	046417	Dai-ichi Life Holdings, Inc.	Japan	42,927,009	-3.17
23	22	058175	MetLife, Inc.	United States	42,034,000	-0.48
24	26	051114	Liberty Mutual Holding Company Inc.	United States	40,624,000	2.03
25	30	058454	Progressive Corporation	United States	40,568,700	7.96

* Percent change is based upon local currency. [1] Premiums shown are earned premiums. [2] AM Best consolidation; U.S. companies only.
Source: Best's Financial Suite-Global; data as of Dec. 13, 2021.

Chapter 1: Industry Overview

another when they move; many independent agents are not licensed in multiple states. Larger insurance organizations may have the resources to track and follow an insured, and they may alert a new agent in the area to where the policyholder has moved.

In addition to agents, the following channels are used to get the business of insurance done:

Brokers: These producers do not necessarily work for an insurance company. Instead, the broker will place policies for clients with the carrier offering the most appropriate rate and coverage terms. The broker is rewarded by the carrier, often at a rate that differs from that paid to the carrier's agents.

Managing General Agents: These individuals or organizations are granted the authority by an insurer to perform a wide array of functions that can include placing business and issuing policies.

Agents are paid commissions based on the value and type of products they sell. Some insurers pay brokers additional compensation based on how the business performs.

Direct Sales: Direct selling of insurance to consumers through mail, internet or telephone solicitations has exploded in recent years. Insurance companies can bypass commissions by removing the agent from the transaction, although marketing and other associated costs can offset the savings.

Increasingly, online relationships are facilitated by traffic aggregators—basically an alternative term for price-comparison sites. The aggregator service links the consumer to the insurer. Aggregator companies receive a commission from product providers when a policy is sold. They also may charge a fee based on any click-through to those providers.

The aggregator service can present challenges on two fronts: The site encourages consumers to select insurance policies based almost exclusively on price, and direct sales are a threat to the independent agent.

Important Functions of Insurance Organizations

Investment: Insurers look to investment managers to make sure they have the funds available to pay claims in a timely manner, match expected losses with investments that mature or become available at appropriate times and help generate income that will contribute to profits. Investment professionals handling insurance assets have an additional constraint: Insurers are prohibited by state regulators from investing too heavily in riskier, more-volatile instrument.

Actuarial: Insurance is based on probability and statistics. Actuaries are skilled in both areas and use their training to help insurers set rates, develop and price policies and coverage, determine reserves for anticipated claims and develop new products that provide coverage at a profit. Actuaries must pass extensive exams to earn their formal designations. Actuaries play influential roles in all sectors of insurance, including property/casualty, life, health and reinsurance. The role of actuaries grows as noninsurance industries—such as hedge funds, risk modelers and capital markets participants—become involved in developing risk products and programs.

www.ambest.com

Chapter 1: Industry Overview

Best's Rankings
Top 10 US Holding Companies – 2023 Edition
Ranked by Assets.
($ 000)

Rank	AMB#	Company Name	2021 Total Assets	2020 Total Assets	% Change
1	058334	Berkshire Hathaway Inc.	958,784,000	873,729,000	9.7%
2	058182	Prudential Financial, Inc.	937,582,000	940,722,000	-0.3%
3	058175	MetLife, Inc.	759,708,000	795,146,000	-4.5%
4	058702	American International Group, Inc.	596,112,000	586,481,000	1.6%
5	058709	Lincoln National Corporation	387,301,000	365,948,000	5.8%
6	055931	Jackson Financial Inc.	375,484,000	353,456,000	6.2%
7	058179	Principal Financial Group, Inc.	304,657,200	296,627,700	2.7%
8	051409	Equitable Holdings, Inc.	292,262,000	275,397,000	6.1%
9	046498	Brighthouse Financial, Inc.	259,840,000	247,869,000	4.8%
10	058106	UnitedHealth Group Incorporated	212,206,000	197,289,000	7.6%

Source: BESTLINK Holding Companies database.

Best's Rankings
Top 10 US Holding Companies – 2023 Edition
Ranked by Revenue.
($ 000)

Rank	AMB#	Company Name	2021 Total Revenue	2020 Total Revenue	% Change
1	058334	Berkshire Hathaway Inc.	354,636,000	286,415,000	23.8%
2	058106	UnitedHealth Group Incorporated	287,597,000	257,141,000	11.8%
3	044026	Cigna Corporation	174,274,000	164,753,000	5.8%
4	058180	Anthem, Inc.	138,639,000	121,867,000	13.8%
5	051149	Centene Corporation	126,801,000	111,595,000	13.6%
6	058052	Humana Inc.	83,596,000	77,155,000	8.3%
7	058182	Prudential Financial, Inc.	71,340,000	57,116,000	24.9%
8	058175	MetLife, Inc.	71,080,000	67,842,000	4.8%
9	058702	American International Group, Inc.	55,101,000	43,736,000	26.0%
10	058312	The Allstate Corporation	50,588,000	41,909,000	20.7%

Source: BESTLINK Holding Companies database.

Chapter 1: Industry Overview

Underwriting: At the heart of insurance is the art and science of assuming risk. Underwriters use a combination of data gathering and analysis, interviewing and professional knowledge to evaluate whether a given risk meets the insurer's standards for prudent evaluation. Their job is to evaluate whether given risks can be covered and, if so, under what terms. Underwriting departments often have the authority to accept or reject risks. Perhaps the most significant responsibility of underwriters is to determine premium that recognizes the likelihood of a claim and enables the insurer to earn a profit. Some of the process has been automated, such as when auto and homeowners insurers access information like driving and property records. Applicants for life insurance and some forms of health coverage may be asked to obtain medical evaluations.

Claims: Sometimes called the "product" that insurance companies deliver, claims are handled by departments that usually operate in two areas: at the offices of the insurer and in the field through claims adjusters. Claims are requests for payment based on losses believed by the policyholder to be covered under an insurance policy. Claims personnel evaluate the request and determine the amount of loss the insurer should pay. Requests for claims payment can come directly to insurers or be handled by agents and brokers working directly with the insured. Claims adjusters can work directly for an insurer or operate as independent businesses that can work for multiple insurers. Claims adjusters often have designated levels of authority to settle claims. Adjusters serve as claims investigators and sometimes conduct elaborate investigations in the event of suspected fraudulent claims.

Insurance Entities

Ownership of traditional insurance companies generally comes in two structures, mutual and stock, although insuring entities may take a number of other forms, including reciprocal exchanges and risk retention groups. **Mutual insurers** are owned by and run for the benefit of their policyholders. Relative to insurance companies with shareholder ownership, mutual insurers have less access to the capital markets to raise money. Many mutual insurance companies have been formed by people or businesses with a common need, such as farmers, firefighters and lumbermen. Mutuals may pay a return of premium or "policyholder dividend" back to the policyholder if the company has strong financial results and a lower-than-expected level of claims. Policyholders also have the ability to vote on company leadership and have a say in certain corporate governance issues.

Reciprocal insurance companies resemble mutual companies. Whereas a mutual insurance company is incorporated, the reciprocal company is run by a management company, referred to as an attorney-in-fact.

Many mutuals were able to grow during the credit crunch of the late 2000s. Their growth is limited, however, because capital has to be generated internally, as there are no shares to sell. Some top former mutual insurance companies, including Metropolitan Life and Prudential, have demutualized to become shareholder-owned public companies. Typically, demutualization is done to raise capital or expand operations. Other companies, including Pacific Life and Liberty Mutual, took an intermediate step and became part of a mutual holding company structure.

www.ambest.com

Chapter 1: Industry Overview

Holding company structures, employed primarily in the U.S., provide easier access to the capital markets, whereby shares can be sold to help raise capital. The holding company owns a significant amount, if not all, of another company's or other companies' common stock. Many insurance companies are part of a holding company structure, with the publicly traded parent company owning stock of the subsidiary or the controlled insurance company or companies.

Captive insurance companies insure the risks of their parent group or groups, and sometimes will insure risks of the group's customers. Captive insurers have become more high profile in recent years after many U.S. states and some international jurisdictions adopted legislation and rules encouraging captives to locate in their domiciles.

Risk retention groups are liability insurance companies owned by policyholders. Membership is limited to people in the same business or activity, which exposes them to similar liability risks. The purpose is to assume and spread liability exposure to members and provide an alternative risk financing mechanism for liability. These entities are formed under the Liability Risk Retention Act of 1986.

Stock companies answer to owners and policyholders. Investment strategies that benefit shareholders—seeking growth and profit—could be carried out to the detriment of policyholders Mutuals, on the other hand, are owned by policyholders, so the focus likely will be on affordability and dividends.

It is difficult to compare profitability generated by public and mutual companies. One thing is certain, however: No particular organizational structure is a cure-all for poorly conceived or executed strategies.

Best's Rankings
Top 20 Global Brokers – 2023 Edition
Ranked by 2021 Total Revenue.
(US$)

2021 Rank	2020 Rank	Broker	2021 Total Revenue
1	1	Marsh McLennan	$19.80 billion
2	2	Aon plc	$12.20 billion
3	3	WTW	$9.00 billion
4	4	Arthur J. Gallagher & Co.	$6.90 billion
5	5	Hub International	$3.23 billion
6	6	Brown & Brown Inc.	$3.05 billion
7	9	Acrisure LLC	$2.97 billion
8	11	Alliant Insurance Services Inc.	$2.90 billion
9	7	Truist Insurance Holdings Inc.	$2.88 billion
10	8	Lockton Inc.	$2.80 billion
11	10	USI Insurance Services LLC	$2.30 billion
12	12	AssuredPartners Inc.	$2.04 billion
13	13	NFP Corp.	$1.90 billion
14	14	Amwins Group Inc.	$1.80 billion
15	15	Howden Group Holdings	$1.57 billion
16	16	The Ardonagh Group	$1.30 billion
17	17	CBIZ Inc.	$1.10 billion
18	18	EPIC Insurance Brokers & Consultants	$806.1 million
19	n/a	AmeriTrust Group Inc.	$667.6 million
20	20	Fanhua Inc.	$513.3 million

Sources: Company information.

Spotlight

Does Insurance Cause Some People to Lie? Behavioral Economics Has the Remedy

Some 24% of consumers think it's acceptable to pad an insurance claim. At least one insurer is fighting back with a new business model.

By understanding and applying the principles of behavioral economics, insurance companies can increase customer satisfaction and ultimately increase profitability, according to a recent study from Celent. Andrew Schwartz, an analyst at Celent and the author of the study, *Applying Behavioral Economics to Insurance*, discussed the findings with AM Best Audio. Following is an edited transcript of the interview.

What is behavioral economics?

The central message of behavioral economics is that humans do not always make rational choices that will maximize utility and that we're often motivated by things like heuristics, which are rules of thumb and biases. However, many of these irrational choices are quite predictable through the application of behavioral economics.

Your study examines why insurance causes some people to lie. Why does it?

The very premise of insurance goes against our present bias heuristic, which means that we tend to value short-term gains. When someone pays a premium and a loss doesn't occur, they might perceive the insurance as an unwise investment because there's no tangible return. As a result, the policyholder may become

www.ambest.com

Spotlight

resentful because they view their insurance policy as a monthly sunk cost rather than as a mitigation tool.

Above all, there is an adversarial business model, because the carrier and the policyholder both are unsatisfied, and they think that the other one's goals are not aligned with theirs. Obviously, for the policyholder, the goal is to pay a policy and quickly become indemnified and made whole in a time of need. For the insurance company, the incentive, and it's not necessarily an evil one, is the perception of the policyholder to probably maximize profitability.

That misalignment leads to some people rationalizing cheating and potentially padding a legitimate claim because they feel like they aren't given the value that they needed. An interesting statistic was that 24% of respondents in an Insurance Research Council poll said they thought it was acceptable to pad an insurance claim by a small amount to make up for deductibles that they're required to pay.

Andrew Schwartz

Are insurers buying into the concept of behavioral economics?

Lemonade has coined themselves a behavioral economics carrier. They have tried to remove the misaligned carrier-policyholder dynamic by changing the fundamental business model. They tell the policyholder that they retain a flat 25% of premiums to cover expenses, 15% is used to cover reinsurance, and the remaining 60% is set aside to settle claims. Their excess profits are donated to a preselected charity, known as their giveback prop. The policyholder can choose from 34 nonprofits, select the one where they want to earmark their excess premium.

That's going to incentivize a more honest claim because the policyholder's cheating the charity of their choosing if they've had a claim. Now if you look at the actual process, it's clear that what Lemonade is doing also is improving the customer experience and reducing fraud.

—John Weber

Listen to the interview with Andrew Schwartz.

Spotlight

Survey: Colleges Need to Better Prepare Future Insurers for Real World

Recruiters and hiring managers who participated in the 2022 *Best's Review* college survey discussed the importance of on-the-job training and developing experience in an insurance education.

Recruiters and hiring managers who participated in the 2022 *Best's Review* college survey say an insurance education must focus on what's necessary for a job that requires a personal touch.

They're happy to give new hires on-the-job training. But insurers want would-be professionals to know what they're doing before they even walk through the door.

"Students also need to be exposed to more types of insurance jobs in the industry rather than focusing on underwriting for the carrier side during their time in school: claims-adjusting, surety, sales, service, actuary, risk managers, etc.," said Ashley Hacker, a client service manager at Gallagher Global Brokerage. That's the message working professionals delivered when they participated in *Best's Review's* 2022 survey of best college insurance programs, saying schools need to do a better job of getting their students ready for the real world and exposing them to the tricks of the trade.

Morgan Wyman, an account executive with CBI Insurance, said she got solid training from Eastern Kentucky University, which was the top vote-getter in

www.ambest.com

Spotlight

the *Best's Review* poll. But she believes that too much of her colleagues' training is focused on areas that don't involve the practical learning that's necessary for a job that requires a personal touch.

"I believe that the educational materials and lessons are excellent and provide students a solid foundation for their future in insurance," she said. "However, I believe it would be beneficial for the students to learn how the concepts and theories they learn relate to real-world, on-the-job scenarios." Wyman said too many of the materials provided to college students focus on theory, but "theories don't always apply if you want to go into claims or sales or something different, so I think they could be doing a better job at that."

"The theories I refer to are those in the CPCU [Chartered Property Casualty Underwriter] courses, which are great," Wyman said. "The CPCU courses pave a clear path for those who want to be more in an underwriting or product development role/career. I think every student should be exposed to these courses, but I think there need to be more classes that highlight other areas in the industry, such as claims, sales, risk management and loss prevention, etc."

While on the job, Wyman said, new insurance professionals should connect to people in underwriting, sales or claims "so they're not spending the majority of the first five to six years in their careers figuring out what exactly they want to do. I think that our graduates, especially at EKU, graduate with a ton of knowledge and a ton of background that could be beneficial at any job, whether it's the agency or company side," she said.

Trey Boggs, an account representative for State Farm in Kentucky and an EKU graduate, said sales is a big part of the industry, and "educating on specific products gives the knowledge to be able to sell those products better, and help people get what they truly need."

EKU graduate Josh Boone, an agent with the Kentucky Farm Bureau, said more real-life situational content can help better prepare students for the challenges they face on any given day. "Learning what a typical day looks like to work in a particular field or position really helps students understand what direction to go once starting a career," Boone said.

Exposing students to the real world also means providing professional services in the classroom, the survey's respondents said. A number of schools provide training and opportunities for taking professional licensing exams, but Wyman said she believes more colleges should allow students to take the licensing exam prior to graduating—without having to take a 20-hour course. "I just wish I could have been licensed without taking the course while I was still in school. I believe interns would be more attractive to employers if they are licensed. Employers often struggle with legal issues having an unlicensed staff member," she said.

Hacker, another EKU grad, recommended that schools improve networking by creating an "accessible Rolodex" of student and alumni contacts in each school to share with other schools. "EKU does already have a Rolodex," she said. "Several school insurance programs are also involved with the Gamma Iota Sigma professional association that may be able to assist in coordinating. I recommend all students join their local chapter since it does provide a wide-scale networking opportunity for students and alumni, but I do think it would be helpful for schools to communicate and have access to all insurance industry contacts outside of GIS as well."

Wyman said an insurance major isn't always very attractive to students. But would-be professionals could develop a passion for the job if they're mentored properly. "Universities that offer a degree in RMI need to figure out how to get students excited about the insurance industry," she said. "From the outside looking in, insurance doesn't seem like it would be a fun and exciting career. But once you're involved, you realize this industry is the exact opposite. It's fun, exciting, competitive and full of amazing people. It is one of the only industries where you get to be hands-on with so many different types of businesses and people."

At Eastern Kentucky University, Wyman said, people from the RMI department went to her classes and "explained the program and how great it was." But she said it initially sounded boring. "But then I took one class, and the only reason why I really loved it was because of the professors," she said. "The professors from that program were the best out of all the departments in the business school. Very hands-on there, 24/7."

—**Tom Davis**

Chapter 2: Property/Casualty

Property/Casualty Market at a Glance

Property/casualty is known as nonlife insurance in many parts of the world. The word "property" usually refers to physical things, including autos, buildings, ships and other concrete items that can be lost, damaged or otherwise become a financial loss to the insured. The word "casualty" usually refers to the concept of liability, and is often associated with coverage of negligent acts or omissions. Some of the largest casualty coverages include auto liability, professional liability, workers' compensation and general liability. The relative size of property/casualty insurers is often gauged by premiums collected.

In the United States, property/casualty insurers file a special statement with the National Association of Insurance Commissioners. The filing is designed to determine premiums and losses by lines of business and to give an accurate view of the insurer's reserving for loss.

As of this publication, AM Best's database contained filing statements for 2,624 total single companies operating in the U.S. property/casualty market. According to the U.S. Department of Labor, 532,000 people work in the property/casualty industry.

According to AM Best's 2022 *Review & Preview* report, the property/casualty industry faces a range of issues.

"Adverse reserve development is a leading cause of insurer insolvency. As a result, reserve adequacy remains a critical rating issue for AM Best. Loss and loss adjusted expense (LAE) reserves are typically the largest liability on a P/C insurer's balance sheet. Underestimating those liabilities may have

Chapter 2: Property/Casualty

a material negative effect on an insurer's reported surplus, potentially resulting in adverse rating action. Unexpected or larger-than-expected changes in an insurer's reserve position may materially affect the assessment of the company's balance sheet strength and enterprise risk management."

On the homeowners segment, AM Best wrote: "Surplus levels continue to support the underlying risks for most U.S. homeowners carriers despite the adverse impact of more frequent and severe weather events, supply chain disruptions and inflationary pressures. ... Key countervailing factors include elevated catastrophe activity and higher reinsurance pricing."

On the auto segment, AM Best wrote: "Most personal auto writers maintain consistently favorable capital positions built on use of newer technology and data analytics to supplement underwriting, claims-handling, and rate-making. ... Distracted driving continues to play a significant part in loss trends and will remain an industry issue. Furthermore, the economic recovery has highlighted a scarcity of qualified truck drivers, which—along with pandemic-related disruptions—has in turn placed strain on quality of the workforce, a factor in claims frequency and severity. However, the growing use of telematics and other technologies are helping transport companies and their insurers address such concerns."

On the surplus lines sector, AM Best wrote: "Insurers remain interested in entering the excess and surplus lines markets, be it through startups, new affiliates in established insurance organizations or a fronting company. Capacity continues to grow, with all indications that expectations remain sensible."

US Property/Casualty – Top Insurers – 2023 Edition
Ranked by 2021 Net Premiums Written.
(US$ Billions)

- State Farm Group (000088)
- Berkshire Hathaway Ins (000811)
- Progressive Ins Group (000780)
- Allstate Ins Group (000008)
- Liberty Mutual Ins Cos (000060)
- Travelers Group (018674)
- USAA Group (004080)
- Chubb INA Group (018498)
- Nationwide Group (005987)
- Farmers Ins Group (000032)

Source: BESTLINK – *Aggregates & Averages Property/Casualty United States & Canada*, 2022 Edition.

www.ambest.com

Chapter 2: Property/Casualty

**US Property/Casualty –
Top Insurers – 2023 Edition**
Ranked by 2021 Gross Premiums Written.
(US$ Billions)

Insurer	Premiums
State Farm Group (000088)	~70
Berkshire Hathaway Ins (000811)	~62
Progressive Ins Group (000780)	~47
Allstate Ins Group (000008)	~42
Liberty Mutual Ins Cos (000060)	~40
Travelers Group (018674)	~32
Chubb INA Group (018498)	~30
USAA Group (004080)	~26
Farmers Ins Group (000032)	~25
Nationwide Group (005987)	~20

Source: *BESTLINK – Aggregates & Averages Property/Casualty United States & Canada*, 2022 Edition.

Property/Casualty Coverage Types and Lines of Business

Property insurance covers damages or loss of property. As a result, rates can be significantly higher in areas susceptible to perils such as hurricanes. Casualty insurance covers indemnity losses and legal expenses from losses such as bodily injury or damage that the policyholder may cause to others.

When a loss occurs, insurance companies establish a claim reserve for the amount of the expected cost of the claim using a projection of estimated loss costs over a period of time. While property reserves are established when a property loss occurs and are usually settled soon after a loss, casualty reserves are established for losses that may not be paid or settled for years (i.e. medical professional liability, workers' compensation, production liability and environmental-related claims). These long-tail lines of business are so named because of the length of time that may elapse before claims are finally settled.

Determining and comparing profitability among property/casualty companies typically is achieved through the combined ratio, which measures the percentage of claims and expenses incurred relative to premiums earned/written. A combined ratio of less than 100 means that the insurer is making an underwriting profit. Companies with combined ratios over 100 still may earn an operating profit, however, because the ratio does not account for investment income.

Property/casualty insurance generally falls into two areas of concentration: personal and commercial lines.

The two largest product lines within the personal lines sector are auto insurance and homeowners insurance.

Chapter 2: Property/Casualty

Commercial lines include insurance for businesses, professionals and commercial establishments. There are many more varieties of commercial lines products than personal lines. The largest two lines are workers' compensation and other liability.

Personal Lines of Business

Personal insurance protects families, individuals and their property, typically homes and vehicles, from loss and damage. Auto and homeowners coverages dominate mostly because of legal provisions that mandate coverage be obtained.

Auto: The largest line of business in the property/casualty sector is auto insurance. According to AM Best's *BestLink* database, the top 50 groups writing auto insurance captured 95% of the total market in 2021, or $247 billion of the $261 billion for all U.S. auto coverage. The largest writer of U.S. private passenger auto is State Farm Group, and the largest writer of all auto coverage overall is now Progressive.

Auto insurance includes collision, liability, comprehensive, personal injury protection and coverage in the event another motorist is uninsured or underinsured.

Homeowners: The second-largest line of personal property/casualty insurance is homeowners, representing $120 billion in direct premiums written for the U.S. property/casualty industry in 2021. Historically, the leading cause of U.S. insured catastrophe losses has been hurricanes and tropical storms, followed by severe thunderstorms and winter storms. The top 50 groups writing homeowners multiperil coverage represented 88% of the U.S. market for homeowners coverage, according to AM Best's *BestLink* database. The largest writer of homeowners multiperil coverage is State Farm Group.

US Property/Casualty – Top Insurers – 2023 Edition

Ranked by 2021 Total Admitted Assets. (US$ Billions)

Berkshire Hathaway Ins (000811)	~53
State Farm Group (000088)	~26
Liberty Mutual Ins Cos (000060)	~11
Travelers Group (018674)	~10
Chubb INA Group (018498)	~8
Allstate Ins Group (000008)	~8
Amer Intl Group (018540)	~7
Progressive Ins Group (000780)	~7
USAA Group (004080)	~6
Nationwide Group (005987)	~5

Source: BESTLINK – *Aggregates & Averages Property/Casualty United States & Canada*, 2022 Edition.

www.ambest.com

Chapter 2: Property/Casualty

**US Property/Casualty –
Top Insurers – 2023 Edition**
Ranked by 2021 Policyholders' Surplus.
(US$ Billions)

Insurer	
Berkshire Hathaway Ins (000811)	~300
State Farm Group (000088)	~145
USAA Group (004080)	~35
Liberty Mutual Ins Cos (000060)	~30
Travelers Group (018674)	~30
Allstate Ins Group (000008)	~25
Amer Intl Group (018540)	~20
Chubb INA Group (018498)	~20
Nationwide Group (005987)	~20
FM Global Group (018502)	~15

Source: BESTLINK – *Aggregates & Averages Property/Casualty United States & Canada*, 2022 Edition.

Commercial Lines of Business

Commercial insurance protects businesses, hospitals, governments, schools and other organizations from losses.

Two of the largest lines in the commercial segment are workers' compensation and general liability.

Workers' Compensation: Insurers on behalf of employers pay benefits regardless of who is to blame for a work-related injury or accident, unless the employee was negligent. In return, the employee gives up the right to sue.

General Liability: General liability insurance protects businessowners (the "insured") from the risks of liabilities imposed by lawsuits and similar claims. Liability insurance is designed to offer its insureds specific protection against third-party insurance claims; in other words, payment is not typically made to the insured, but rather to someone suffering loss but who is not a party to the insurance contract. In general, damages caused by intentional acts are not covered under general liability insurance policies. When a claim is made, the insurance carrier has the duty to defend the insured.

Other major lines of business in the property/casualty commercial sector include:

Aircraft (all perils): Often excluded under standard commercial general liability forms. Coverage for aircraft liability loss exposure can include hull (physical damage) and medical payments coverages.

Allied Lines: Coverage for loss of or damage to real or personal property by reason other than fire. Losses from wind and hail, water (sprinkler, flood, rain), civil disorder and damage by aircraft or vehicles are included.

Chapter 2: Property/Casualty

Boiler and Machinery: Coverage for damage to boilers, pressure vessels and machinery.

Burglary and Theft: Coverage to protect against burglary, theft, forgery, counterfeiting, fraud and the like. Protection can include on- and off-premises exposure.

Commercial Auto: Coverage to protect against financial loss because of legal liability for injury to

US Property/Casualty – Top Lines – 2023 Edition
Ranked by 2021 Direct Premiums Written.
(US$ 000)

Business Line	Direct Premiums Written
Private Passenger Auto Liability	$152,905,405
Homeowners Multiple Peril	118,522,901
Private Passenger Auto Physical Damage	108,607,215
Other Liability – Occurrence	64,018,283
Workers' Compensation	52,153,460
Other Liability – Claims-Made	41,708,212
Commercial Auto Liability	41,448,677
Commercial Multiple Peril – Non-Liability	32,641,483
Inland Marine	29,728,393
Fire	18,799,492
Allied Lines	18,052,680
Commercial Multiple Peril – Liability	17,319,158
Multiple Peril Crop	14,888,372
Commercial Auto Physical Damage	12,347,351
Medical Professional Liability	10,904,410
Surety	7,434,087
Mortgage Guaranty	5,715,829
Farmowners Multiple Peril	4,976,320
Group Accident & Health	4,955,267
Ocean Marine	4,653,061
Products Liability	4,428,399
Warranty	4,054,573
Earthquake	3,875,609
Federal Flood	3,139,626
Aircraft	2,530,479
Credit	2,488,377
Boiler & Machinery	2,392,001
Other Accident & Health	2,188,560
Fidelity	1,421,920
Other Lines	1,319,208
Excess Workers' Compensation	1,313,617
Private Crop	1,267,702
Private Flood	1,005,774
Burglary & Theft	475,070
Financial Guaranty	398,015
Credit Accident & Health	182,172
International	52,649
Total Property/Casualty Industry	**$794,313,842**

Note: Data for some companies in this report has been received from the NAIC. Reflects Grand Total (includes Canada and U.S. Territories).
Source: BESTLINK — *State/Line (P/C Lines) - P/C, US*; Data as of: June 11, 2022.

www.ambest.com

Chapter 2: Property/Casualty

persons or damage to property of others caused by the insured's commercial motor vehicle.

Commercial Multiple Peril: Commercial insurance coverage combining two or more property, liability and/or risk exposures.

Fidelity: Coverage for employee theft of money, securities or property, written with a per-loss limit, a per-employee limit or a per-position limit. Employee dishonesty coverage is one of the key coverages provided in a commercial crime policy.

Financial Guaranty: Credit protection for investors in municipal bonds, commercial mortgage-backed securities and auto or student loans. Provides financial recourse in the event of a default on the bond or other instrument.

Fire: Coverage for loss of or damage to real or personal property due to fire or lightning. Losses from interruption of business and loss of other income from these sources are included.

Inland Marine: Coverage for goods in transit and goods, such as construction equipment, subject to frequent relocation.

Medical Professional Liability: Protects against failure to use due care and the standard of care expected from a doctor, dentist, nurse, hospital or other health-related organization.

Mortgage Guaranty: Insurance against financial loss because of nonpayment of principal, interest and other amounts agreed to be paid under the terms of a note, bond or other evidence of indebtedness that is secured by real estate.

Multiple Peril Crop: Protects against losses caused by crop yields that are too low. This line was developed initially by the U.S. Department of Agriculture.

Ocean Marine: Provides protection for all types of oceangoing vessels and their cargo, as well as legal liability of owners and shippers.

Products Liability: Protection against loss arising out of legal liability because of injury or damage resulting from the use of a product or the liability of a contractor after a job is completed.

Surety: Guarantee that the principal of a bond will act in accordance with the terms established by the bond.

Spotlight

Automakers Build New Insurance Future

As data and technology pervade the car manufacturing industry, automakers have made fresh inroads into insurance.

For more than a century, carmakers and automobile insurers have largely kept to their own lanes. That was before data ruled. In 2022 data and technology have inspired the automobile industry to get more involved in the insurance side of the ledger, prompting an increase in the number of interindustry partnerships and more.

For auto insurers, partnerships and other steps car manufacturers have taken to edge their way into the insurance industry offer a way to gain and maintain market share in the highly competitive personal auto space, AM Best Senior Director Richard Attanasio said. Offering products directly and at the point of a vehicle sale brings carriers an avenue of distribution with potentially lower expense levels and additional insight that can help set rates, he said.

Insurers working closely with manufacturers agree that they benefit from access to new data and driving behaviors, and how that impacts losses as automation advances and interest in electric vehicles surges. And carmakers who establish their own insurance operations can acquire a "natural feedback loop on driving patterns, effectiveness of safety features, etc., which allows them to further hone their product to meet customer expectations," Attanasio said.

Points of entry vary by manufacturer and even by country. For instance, Tesla progressed from

www.ambest.com

Spotlight

broker to fronting agency partner to insurance subsidiary. Swiss Re and BMW collaborated to craft a vehicle-specific insurance rating parameter for primary carriers globally to calculate premiums. Some carmakers, like Toyota, are building out insurance brokerages. Others teamed up with carriers on embedded products.

Toyota overtook Ford as the leading car brand in the U.S. in 2021, based on 1.9 million vehicle sales, according to market and consumer data company Statista. Ford had 1.8 million, followed by Chevrolet's 1.5 million. Nationwide has partnered with the top two, as well as startup electric "adventure" vehicle Rivian.

Nationwide gains knowledge and strengthens trust by expanding original equipment manufacturer partnerships, said Senior Vice President of Corporate Development Angie Klett, creating "a relationship within their ecosystem that builds upon the customer having the say, the power and determining the path of an experience." Carmakers and insurance partners today take a customer-first approach that varies from company to company, said Klett. Choose a manufacturing partner carefully, she advised, with an eye on aligning values and strategies.

> For auto insurers, partnerships and other steps car manufacturers have taken to edge their way into the insurance industry offer a way to gain and maintain market share in the highly competitive personal auto space.

Richard Attanasio

Each side decides direction for the insurance product, such as if, how and when to embed insurance in the buying process. Klett said embedding is most strategic for manufacturers with a niche market, where customers think a company like Tesla or Rivian has a better handle on the needs of their vehicles' owners. "They're direct-to-consumer OEMs. The buying, the servicing is different. It's not the same as a Ford or Toyota," said Klett.

Specialized manufacturers, such as Rivian, are notably invested in streamlining the entire car-owning experience, said Sarah Jacobs, Nationwide vice president of personal lines product development, and will lean into the process.

Toyota Financial Services is an owner of independent property/casualty insurance agency Toyota Insurance Management Solutions (TIMS), which distributes product from multiple carriers. Will Nicklas, president of Toyota Insurance, acknowledged manufacturers' earlier reluctance to enter the highly competitive auto insurance market in the United States.

"But I think when we decided that cars were going to be connected, and there were going to be a lot more services that we could provide to customers, it made a lot of sense," he said. "When you think about how insurance plays a role in car ownership, every six months, maybe every 12 months, a customer is renewing an insurance policy. We saw it as a gap in the ownership experience."

Nicklas thinks of TIMS as "this new, connected tissue, or this glue that's bringing these two industries together" for a "really powerful collaboration."

According to the TIMS website, working with Toyota companies and external partners allows the broker to harness data and technology to "improve safety, convenience and save customers time and money."

The Counterpoint

Some insurance industry experts think the partnerships are helping carriers and manufacturers, but they doubt Tesla will inspire other carmakers to become underwriters. They cite the complexity of regulatory approvals, particularly in the United States, and profit and loss swings in auto, even among large, legacy insurers.

Risk Information Inc. Editor Brian Sullivan put it bluntly: "There is no advantage at all to a traditional auto manufacturer owning a traditional insurance company."

Jacobs said regulatory work can't be underestimated. Insurance is "very challenging to break into."

Barriers are a little easier to clear in some other countries, particularly with a carrier partner. Volkswagen Autoversicherung AG was founded in 2013 as a joint venture between Allianz Versicherungs-AG and Volkswagen Financial Services AG. Volkswagen Autoversicherung AG offers auto insurance in Germany as a primary insurer. In about 30 other countries or markets VW is an insurance broker, the company said.

"The technology of the cars, especially the car data, gain an increasing importance for the development of our motor insurance products," a Volkswagen spokesperson said. "For example, in Germany the safety features of the cars have a direct influence on the motor insurance pricing." The company hopes to gain telematics experience and integrate insurance offers into VW onboard systems.

Brandy Mayfield, senior vice president and managing director, digital economy for Aon, said partnerships between manufacturers and insurers offer an attractive middle ground.

"As manufacturers build differentiated products, they want to make sure carriers have capacity to insure newer/different technology. Manufacturers also want to minimize friction in the insurance purchase journey and create continued revenue streams from their buyers," she said.

On the other hand, she said, "shifting from acting as a broker to an insurer presents a significant leap in terms of regulatory complexity, capital intensity and moving the brand into a new category with mixed views from consumers."

"For original equipment manufacturers to make that investment there will have to be a clear opportunity to differentiate from traditional insurers or meet truly unmet needs in the marketplace," she added. "Carmakers must determine what they're solving for by setting up their own insurance structure: more clients, a differentiated insurance product, etc. Many also want to capitalize on profits from the insurance space."

Spotlight

Carriers can grow a book for certain auto types more rapidly than in the traditional market, she said. Customers may get improved access to parts and repair services, increasing satisfaction with insurers and carmakers. Doubly important for newer vehicles with limited production is "a network to quickly obtain parts and repair," said Mayfield.

Tesla's push into insurance was reported to be motivated by reducing the cost of ownership. Repair costs ran higher because fewer technicians are familiar with the connected, electric vehicle. Tesla was known for supply chain challenges even before the pandemic, extending repair times.

"Other manufacturers could take a similar approach and offer insurance directly," Attanasio said, although it would require a significant amount of industry knowledge and infrastructure, including a high level of product/pricing sophistication and policy administration and claims capabilities.

Entrepreneur Elon Musk drew distinctions between how automaker Tesla Motors' insurance operations cover auto risk compared to the traditional insurance industry, which he said suffers from too many players extracting part of the premium along the insurance value chain. "Insurance is quite significant," said Musk, Tesla's chief executive officer. "The car insurance thing is a bigger deal than it may seem. A lot of people are paying 30%, 40% as much as their lease payment for the car, in car insurance." Tesla said its real-time insurance is based on measurable driving behavior.

"There is no advantage at all to a traditional auto manufacturer owning a traditional insurance company."

Brian Sullivan

Technology Roots

Twenty-two years ago, when OnStar was collecting vehicle usage data in 34 of General Motors' then-54 models, a spokesman said the onboard automobile information system was working on partnering with insurers. OnStar's inducement included cost savings because insurers wouldn't need to develop data-gathering equipment and then get it into vehicles.

That was three years before Progressive Corp.—which has since become the third-largest private passenger writer in the United States, according to AM Best data—piloted a usage-based insurance program to research driving habits. In 2008, Progressive started offering customers the option of tying driving data to premiums.

Telematics adoption lagged through the years, even as the ease improved from the early days, when consumers were required to install dongles to access UBI. Now that smartphones are common, telematics options from multiple carriers are just an app away. The amount of information an insurer can gather comes close to carmaker-installed monitoring systems, said Sullivan.

Mayfield, however, raised a prime consumer concern: data privacy. "Dealership agents should be prepared to answer a similar line of questioning from consumers: What information from their vehicles will manufacturers plan to share with insurance companies?"

That's a problem for carmakers because the distribution system incentivizes salespeople to sell vehicles as quickly and with as little friction as possible, said Sullivan. "All a salesperson wants is to get the car off the lot. Anything that might get in the way of closing the sale immediately will be ignored by sales and finance people in dealerships. Insurance is far more complicated than selling rust protection add-ons."

Connected carmakers are already collecting enormous amounts of data on how vehicles are driven and maintained. That can give them an edge, albeit a minor one, as telematics becomes more widely accepted, according to Sullivan, even as many car buyers opt to retain a degree of privacy, or at least the right to decide who has access to their personal movements and habits, and when.

Ford affiliate American Road Services Co. offers Ford Insure, underwritten by Nationwide Mutual Insurance Co. and its affiliates. Ford Insure customers employ FordPass App, which is compatible with smartphones, and FordPass Connect, an optional feature on some of the carmaker's models—on newer vehicles to transmit data on miles driven, hard braking, accelerating, and stop-and-go and night driving.

Ford's insurance messaging mirrors that of partner Nationwide for the general public. "While that discount is being calculated, you automatically get a 10% discount just for signing up," Ford Insure notes on its website, promoting auto insurance discounts as high as 40% and potential additional savings by bundling other vehicles, home or pet insurance with auto coverage.

Jacobs thinks 70% of new customers will opt in to UBI plans within five years, based on current trends.

Sullivan isn't surprised, seeing the day when drivers who decline to use telematics are presumed to be high-mileage or high-risk policyholders. Even if they're not, they will pay more for the privilege of privacy, he predicted.

—Renée Kiriluk-Hill

Spotlight

Insurance Coverage Questions Surround Emerging NIL Industry

The name, image and likeness environment in college sports is compared to the wild, Wild West, and this includes the insurance aspect.

In the world of big college sports, things don't always play out the way they're supposed to. The star pitcher for your university's baseball team can lock up a name, image and likeness (NIL) deal, then get benched after a few bad outings. "How do you insure that?" Stephens Insurance Senior Vice President and General Counsel Patrick McAlpine asked. The answer is different depending on the state, and it's part of what former University of Kansas football player Pat Brown describes as "the wild, Wild West."

The rules are the result of *O'Bannon v. NCAA*, a 2009 lawsuit brought against the National Collegiate Athletic Association by former UCLA basketball player Ed O'Bannon, who sought compensation for use of his NIL in a video game. His victory opened the door for other athletes to be compensated, and the NIL world exploded in 2021 with the emergence of collectives—groups of alumni and boosters who are not associated with the university—that arrange NIL deals with athletes.

"These individuals or entities are just collectively working together, and there's no real governing structure," McAlpine said. "That makes it really hard to insure anything if there's not an entity, a corporation, an LLC or something like that because underwriters are immediately going to have problems with an unincorporated group of people, especially doing something novel like this."

Brown, now director of risk management & insurance and an investment adviser for Edmonds Duncan, said athletes have to be concerned about getting injured, and they also have to be aware that they may now be a target because of the money they make. "If an athlete gets into a scenario where he or she signs a contract, but then they don't fulfill the obligation, is that company going to come after that athlete?" Brown said. "In this litigious society that we are in, I can certainly see something like that happening."

Another question concerns the issue of catastrophic injury coverage for athletes. The NCAA, which oversees the governance of college sports, has disability insurance in place for "exceptional student athletes" playing at member institutions who obtain pre-approved financing, according to the NCAA's website. It protects them against future loss as a professional athlete, and is administered by three subsidiaries of Tokio Marine HCC.

Brown said he wonders if the emergence of NIL money will impact scholarship and Pell Grant money to the point where the student-athlete will be on their own to get insurance.

Sean Clifford, a current Penn State University football player who founded Limitless NIL to help student athletes navigate their way through this new frontier, said there is currently no issue with the NCAA program. He can see the potential issues.

In January 2022, Stephens Insurance announced that it had reached an NIL deal with University of Arkansas linebacker Bumper Pool. "In Arkansas, our NIL law says that we actually have to continue payments for the contracted period, even if they don't play, they get hurt or they leave the team," McAlpine said. "You have to structure your contract to take into account for that, at some cost."

—Anthony Bellano

Chapter 3: Life & Annuity

Life Market at a Glance

Life/health insurers cover the risks of dying, offer retirement savings products and provide a variety of protections against disability, specific types of illness and more. As of this publication, AM Best's database contained annual filings for 1,966 total single combined life & health companies operating in the United States. Life insurers often have longer investment and coverage horizons because retirement and mortality are often events that are decades away. The relative size of life/health insurers is often gauged by assets under management. Life insurers have increasingly embraced annuities and other forms of retirement savings, as sales of traditional life products have been flat or grown modestly, although this trend has reversed somewhat since COVID-19, and baby boomers transition into retirement.

The U.S. life/health industry recorded $645 billion in total premiums and $5 trillion in total cash and invested assets as of 2021, the most recent full year available. Lines of business include individual life, group life, individual annuities, group annuities, supplemental contracts, credit life, industrial life, group accident & health, credit accident & health and other accident & health.

According to the 2022 edition of *Best's Aggregates & Averages, Life/Health, United States and Canada*, Prudential of America Group leads the list of largest life/health industry groups and unaffiliated single companies with $707 billion in total admitted assets as of year-end 2021.

Risk Profile

The risk profile of life insurance is very different from that of property/casualty insurance. Life insurance

Chapter 3: Life & Annuity

Best's Rankings

Top 10 US Life/Health Companies – 2023 Edition
Ranked by 2021 Direct Premiums Written.
(US$ 000)

Rank	Company Name	AMB#	Direct Premiums Written
1	UnitedHealth Life Companies	069973	55,548,345
2	Aetna Life Group	070202	41,263,331
3	Prudential of America Group	070189	40,071,744
4	Massachusetts Mutual Life Group	069702	37,889,900
5	MetLife Life Ins Companies	070192	36,645,192
6	New York Life Group	069714	34,980,851
7	Lincoln Finl Group	070351	28,130,421
8	Northwestern Mutual Group	069515	23,546,581
9	Cigna Life Group	070173	23,536,708
10	Athene US Life Group	070478	23,314,094

Top 10 US Life/Health Companies – 2023 Edition
Ranked by 2021 Net Premiums Written.
(US$ 000)

Rank	Company Name	AMB#	Net Premiums Written
1	UnitedHealth Life Companies	069973	56,244,294
2	Prudential of America Group	070189	45,960,754
3	New York Life Group	069714	34,621,033
4	Aetna Life Group	070202	29,926,933
5	MetLife Life Ins Companies	070192	26,774,801
6	Massachusetts Mutual Life Group	069702	25,285,698
7	Cigna Life Group	070173	22,938,914
8	Northwestern Mutual Group	069515	22,551,259
9	AIG Life & Retirement Group	070342	22,248,353
10	Jackson Natl Group	069578	20,024,506

Top 10 US Life/Health Companies – 2023 Edition
Ranked by 2021 Total Admitted Assets.
(US$ 000)

Rank	Company Name	AMB#	Total Admitted Assets
1	Prudential of America Group	070189	707,207,343
2	MetLife Life Ins Companies	070192	461,437,117
3	New York Life Group	069714	392,916,326
4	Massachusetts Mutual Life Group	069702	365,446,331
5	TIAA Group	070362	360,223,526
6	AIG Life & Retirement Group	070342	345,824,628
7	Northwestern Mutual Group	069515	334,756,177
8	Lincoln Finl Group	070351	334,508,148
9	Jackson Natl Group	069578	321,914,245
10	John Hancock Life Insurance Group	069542	309,176,249

Top 10 US Life/Health Companies – 2023 Edition
Ranked by 2021 Capital & Surplus.
(US$ 000)

Rank	Company Name	AMB#	Capital & Surplus
1	TIAA Group	070362	42,972,680
2	Northwestern Mutual Group	069515	29,283,152
3	Massachusetts Mutual Life Group	069702	26,268,606
4	New York Life Group	069714	22,616,667
5	Prudential of America Group	070189	20,136,840
6	MetLife Life Ins Companies	070192	19,078,958
7	State Farm Life Group	070126	15,542,718
8	Thrivent Finl for Lutherans	006008	13,694,795
9	AIG Life & Retirement Group	070342	12,470,936
10	Pacific Life Group	069720	11,353,204

Source: BESTLINK AM Best data.

Chapter 3: Life & Annuity

is generally more asset-intensive, and most product liabilities have a substantially longer duration.

The main purpose of life insurance is to cover the risk of dying too early or, in the case of annuities, the risks that may come with living longer than expected. Policies help beneficiaries maintain their standard of living after the policyholder dies. They also can protect beneficiaries and insureds from the possibility of outliving their assets.

While some types of life insurance include a savings component that can provide retirement income, life insurance itself isn't necessarily an investment. But for insurance companies, and especially life insurers, profitability is largely dependent on investment performance. In general, life insurers have enough data surrounding life expectancies and risk classes to determine rates and to accurately predict claims.

Because a policy can remain in effect for decades, life insurers' obligations tend to be relatively long term. As a result, many insurers invest in longer-duration assets such as long-term bonds and real estate.

Life Insurers Chasing Wider Range of Opportunities

AM Best's annual *Review & Preview* report details a range of key trends shaping the future for life/annuity insurers.

Companies continue to characterize COVID-19 mortality as having an earnings impact as opposed to a balance sheet impact, suggesting no significant changes to reserves. Most carriers continue to experience higher mortality rates than usual, resulting in slightly favorable developments for long-term care. In 2021, mortality was higher for working-age populations, which affected both individual and group life claims. Some carriers playing both sides of the equation also benefited from the longevity impact. To date, the long-term implications of COVID-19 mortality on liabilities and future pricing assumptions appear minimal. However, questions remain about mortality due to other causes, illnesses and conditions.

COVID-19 forced carriers to use more digitized approaches to underwriting. Big Data in the life/annuity segment continues to improve, leading to more-advanced underwriting standards. AM Best expects to see more granularity and underwriting capabilities on the mortality front for both life and longevity insurance. Actuaries typically benefit from large data sets that have stood the test of time. Although historical data is by no means indicative of the future, it does help actuaries frame a problem to understand the order of magnitude and sense of direction of a certain situation. Modeling can support informed decisions, but the type, quality and timeliness of data used remain challenges.

Life/annuity insurers' business profiles have changed rapidly the past couple of years. Companies have been de-risking their liability profiles since the financial crisis of 2008-2009. Actions such as divesting in-force legacy blocks and cutting back or discontinuing sales of higher capital-intensive or interest-sensitive products (universal life products with secondary guarantees, variable annuities with living benefits, fixed deferred annuities with high minimum guaranteed crediting rates) have accelerated the past two years. More life/

Chapter 3: Life & Annuity

annuity insurers have exited from the individual life and annuity lines of business, and there has been a considerable increase in divestments and block reinsurance transactions recorded during this time, although AM Best has expected to see a trend the other way for some insurers given the higher prevailing interest rate environment.

The industry has seen its share of M&A and startups over the past few years. Capital efficiency and improved asset management have been common themes. Many on-site companies—especially publicly traded companies that focus on buybacks and returns on equity—have attempted to offload capital-intensive businesses. The supply of capital has risen to meet this demand, with many new players entering the capital-intensive liability space.

There have typically been a few common themes among the capital providers. Private equity players with an ability to source and manage fixed-income assets have established a presence in Bermuda. Many players want to put capital and fixed-income assets to work, and long-term capital-intensive liabilities have been an avenue of choice for them. These lines of businesses include fixed annuities, variable annuities, pension risk transfer, and universal life with secondary guarantees. New entrants typically have expertise to manage and source fixed-income assets, which they use in their overall portfolio. In this macroeconomic environment, every competitive advantage players can leverage counts.

Life/annuity carriers began to market fixed-indexed linked annuities (FILAs) in 2021. This new and innovative product should not be confused with the RILA or buffer annuity, a variable annuity that can be sold only by SEC-registered advisers. The FILA captures some of the appeal of the RILA by allowing policyholders to expose some of the credited interest to market risk for the chance to achieve higher gains. The FILA is not an SEC-registered product because it does not put the principal at risk.

US Life/Health – Asset Distribution (2021)
($000)

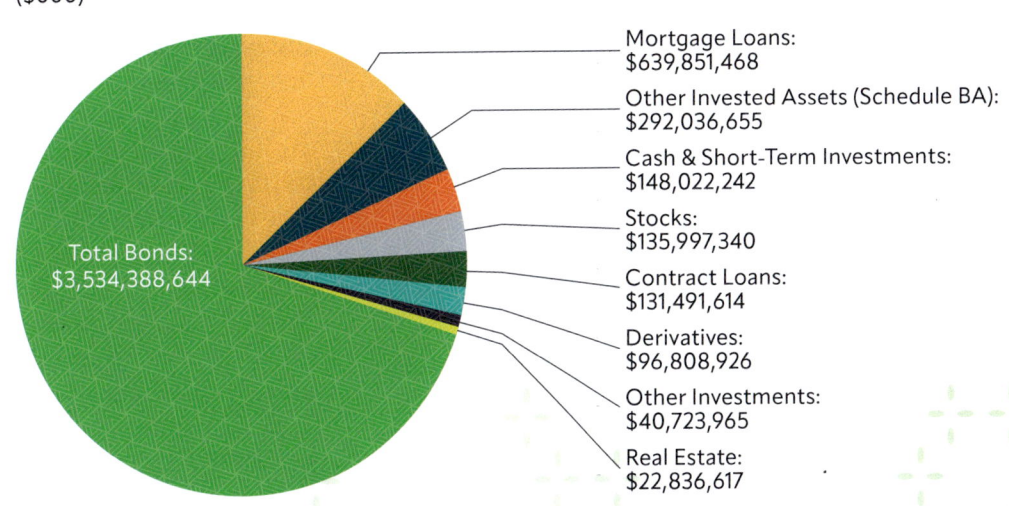

- Total Bonds: $3,534,388,644
- Mortgage Loans: $639,851,468
- Other Invested Assets (Schedule BA): $292,036,655
- Cash & Short-Term Investments: $148,022,242
- Stocks: $135,997,340
- Contract Loans: $131,491,614
- Derivatives: $96,808,926
- Other Investments: $40,723,965
- Real Estate: $22,836,617

Source: BESTLINK – *Aggregates & Averages Life/Health United States & Canada*, 2022 Edition. Securities are reported on the basis prescribed by the National Association of Insurance Commissioners.

www.ambest.com

Chapter 3: Life & Annuity

Another product innovation came when BlackRock Inc. teamed with Brighthouse and Equitable Holdings to provide an annuity option in a new target-date retirement product for 401(k) plans. Called LifePath Paycheck solution, the annuity option provides retirees with a guaranteed stream of income for life by allowing them to use up to 30% of their 401(k) balance to purchase the annuity.

In their ongoing search for growth, life/annuity insurers are engaging with consumers in new ways and diversifying their overall distribution strategies. In an AM Best survey on distribution in the segment, 35% of respondents said that direct-to-consumer (DTC) was the channel most under consideration to develop. The move to DTC is part of an overall strategy for many insurers to use a multichannel approach rather than the traditional independent or career agents to market their products.

Important Lines of Life Business and Products

Life insurers market a variety of life products that range from simple to complex.

Total Life, In Force & Issued: The size of a life company can be measured by the face amount of its portfolio—that is, the amount of life insurance it has issued as well as the amount in force. In force is the total face amount of insurance outstanding at a point in time. Issued measures the face amount of policies an insurer has sold within a given time period.

Permanent Life: Permanent life provides death benefits and cash value in return for periodic payments. Cash surrender value, or nonforfeiture value, is the sum of money an insurance company will pay a policyholder who decides to cancel the policy before its expiration or before the policyholder's death. Over the long term, these products usually produce solid, sustainable profitability that is derived from adequate pricing, underwriting and investment returns. Permanent life products include whole life, universal life and variable universal life.

Whole Life: Whole life pays a death benefit and also accumulates a cash value. These have a high initial expense strain for the issuing company due to large first-year commissions to agents, who get a percentage of premiums. Over time, whole life provides an income stream to the company and the agent. It carries premium, death benefit and cash value guarantees that other products don't provide.

Universal Life: These are flexible premium policies that incorporate a savings element. The cash values that are accumulated are put into investments with the intention of earning more in interest. Those accumulations can be used to reduce later premiums or to build up the cash value. For companies offering this product, the premium payment flexibility adds an element of uncertainty, as does the potential for changing market conditions that can affect interest rates. The next generation of this product line, universal life with secondary guarantees, offers competitive rates while providing long-term premium and death benefit guarantees, regardless of actual performance. The tight pricing and high reserve requirements can limit profitability. Indexed universal life is now the most popular iteration of universal life.

Chapter 3: Life & Annuity

Variable Universal Life: These flexible premium policies allow for investment of the cash value into mutual fund-like accounts the insurance carrier holds in separate accounts rather than in its general account. Because policy values will vary based on the performance of investments, these policies present an investment risk to the policyholder. Rather than having a monthly addition to the cash value based on a declared interest-crediting rate, the accumulated cash value of the variable policy is adjusted daily to reflect the investment experience of the funds selected. Insurers can be susceptible to profit fluctuations because of the equity market's effect on mutual fund fees. In addition, the insurer lacks control over separate account assets, and policyholder behavior may impact profitability.

Term Life: Term life provides protection for a specified period of time. It pays a benefit only if the insured's death occurs during the coverage period. It can be considered a pure protection product and a consumer's entry-level life insurance product. Term periods typically range from one year to 30 years, although there are annually renewable policies, which are designed for longer durations. Term life, which is a highly competitive product, is marketed through many traditional distribution channels, as well as through financial institutions, banks and various direct distribution channels including the internet. More recent products offer long-term premium guarantees, where the premium is guaranteed to be the same for a given period of years. Return of premium (ROP) term products have also become popular of late, offering policyowners a refund of all premiums paid if the insured is still alive at the end of the term period. Concerns to insurers include high lapse rates, compressed margins and high reserve requirements.

Group Life: Generally in the form of term life, group life is marketed to employers or association groups. The cost also may be shared by the participant and the master policyholder, usually the employee and employer, respectively. Typically, an initial benefit level may be paid by the employer, and, in some cases, employees may elect to pay for additional coverage. As with term life, competition is intense.

Annuity Products

Insurance companies provide annuities, which, at their most basic, are contracts that ensure an income stream. A payment or series of payments is made to an insurance company, and in return, the insurer agrees to pay an income for a specified time period. Annuities can take many forms but have a couple of basic properties: an immediate or deferred payout with fixed (guaranteed) or variable returns. Consequently, different annuity types can resemble certificates of deposit, pensions or even investment portfolios.

Challenges to the Annuity Industry

Life insurance companies must minimize the risk of disintermediation. This happens when deferred annuity holders seeking higher-yielding alternatives withdraw funds prematurely (often during periods of increasing interest rates), and force companies to pay these surrenders by liquidating investments that may be in an unrealized loss position. Insurers can mitigate this risk by matching the duration of its interest-sensitive liability portfolio with the duration of its asset portfolio, and by selling a diversified portfolio of products. Insurers also mitigate risk

www.ambest.com

Chapter 3: Life & Annuity

by designing deferred annuities with market-value adjustments on surrender values.

Immediate Annuities: These annuities are designed to guarantee owners a predetermined income stream on a monthly, quarterly, semiannual or annual basis in exchange for a lump sum. Options are limited from the annuity holder's perspective, so profits are generally less volatile in the short term.

Best's Rankings
Top US Life Reinsurers – 2023 Edition
Ranked by 2021 Individual Life Insurance In Force.

AMB#	Company Name	Individual Amount in Force ($ 000)
009080	RGA Reinsurance Company	1,778,685,283
007283	Swiss Re Life & Health America Inc.	1,760,361,768
070253	SCOR Life US Group	1,700,933,330
006746	Munich American Reassurance Company	1,221,833,669
068031	Hannover Life Reassurance Co of America	1,210,828,591
006234	General Re Life Corporation	288,295,764
009791	Canada Life Assurance Company USB	245,332,693
061745	PartnerRe Life Reinsurance Co of America	104,787,766
060560	Wilton Reassurance Company	90,881,557
008863	Optimum Re Insurance Company	85,608,548
006976	Employers Reassurance Corporation	70,640,865
009096	M Life Insurance Company	61,571,521

Source: BESTLINK

However, the long-term nature of these products exposes the insurer to reinvestment risk and longevity risk.

Group Annuities: These differ slightly from individual annuities in that the payout is dependent on the life expectancy of all members of the group rather than on one individual. Many company retirement plans, such as 401(k) plans, are annuities that will pay a regular income to the retiree. Tax-deferred annuity plans—403(b) and 457 plans—utilize group annuities as the investment vehicle for participant contributions.

Deferred Annuities: Deferred annuities are a type of long-term savings product that allows assets to grow tax-deferred until annuitization.

Fixed-Deferred Annuities: These products guarantee a minimum rate of interest during the time the account is growing and typically guarantee a minimum benefit upon annuitization.

For the issuer, fixed annuities are subject to significant asset/liability mismatch risks, as described above. Also, when interest rates fall, spread earnings—or the difference between the yield on investments and credited rates—can decrease, and asset cash flows must be reinvested at lower rates.

Fixed-Indexed Annuities: These products are credited with a return that is based on changes in an equity index. The insurance company typically guarantees a minimum return. Payouts may be periodic or in a lump sum. The potential for gains is an attractive feature during favorable market conditions; however, gains may not be as favorable as those available from variable annuities or straight equity investments. Sales of these products may decline if equity markets go through a prolonged downturn or a prolonged upturn.

Variable Annuities: The participant is given a range of investment options, typically mutual funds, from which to choose. The rate of return on the purchase payment, and the amount of the periodic payments, will vary depending on the performance of the selected investments and the level of expense charges in the product.

Variable annuity sales tend to slump during unfavorable equity market conditions. In addition, the primary sources of revenue for these products are account value-based fees, which also decline when market conditions deteriorate. Relatively thin margins, increasing product complexity (e.g. guaranteed living benefits) and volatile capital requirements put variable annuities at the riskier end of the product continuum, from the standpoint of the issuing insurer.

Because variable annuities allow for investments in equity and fixed-income securities, they are regulated by the U.S. Securities and Exchange Commission. Fixed annuities and fixed-indexed annuities are not securities and, as such, are not regulated by the SEC.

Registered Index-Linked Annuities: A hybrid between a variable annuity and a fixed-indexed annuity, these products offer somewhat more of an upside growth potential than traditional fixed-indexed annuities in exchange for a certain level of downside risk, although less than traditional variable annuities. As registered products, they can only be sold by FINRA-registered representatives.

Accident & Health Products

Credit Accident & Health: This insurance covers a borrower for accidental injury, disability and related health expenses. It is designed specifically to make monthly payments until the insured can recover and resume earning income to repay the debt. If an individual is totally disabled for the life of the loan, the policy would pay the remaining balance, in most cases, but only one month at a time.

Group Accident & Health: These plans are designed for a natural group, such as employees of a single employer, or union members, and their dependents. Insurance is provided under a single policy, with individual certificates issued to each participant.

Other Accident & Health: Products that fall into this category could be policies for individuals that cover major medical, disability insurance, long-term care, dental, dread disease or auxiliary coverages such as Medicare supplement.

Spotlight

Staid Annuities Get Star Treatment in Movie About the Importance of Guaranteed Retirement Income

The Baby Boomer Dilemma, a documentary film by Doug Orchard, tells how annuities in retirement portfolios can guard against "haircuts" to traditional pensions or Social Security benefits, as well as potential volatility in defined contribution plans.

Ever ponder exactly what it means for filmmakers to have their movies obtain a rating from the Motion Picture Association? Probably not.

But for documentarian Doug Orchard, that was a key question for his film *The Baby Boomer Dilemma*, which explores shortcomings in the current retirement system and the role of annuities within portfolios. Securing the film's PG rating meant it could be shown in theaters, but he said it also carried another kind of status—an imprimatur from the MPA that the film wasn't just an infomercial or long-form sales pitch for a financial product.

In fact, it's the first movie about annuities to be rated by the MPA. The film's website describes the movie as "an exposé of America's retirement experiment." It had a limited theatrical release in late 2021 and is available for streaming.

"I had a model in my mind going in, and my model for the framework of this film was I wanted to do a deep

AM BEST SINCE 1899

Spotlight

dive into pensions, I wanted to do a deep dive into Social Security, I wanted to do a whole deep dive into the deferred comp plans—which is where most people put their money—and then I wanted to do a deep dive into annuities," Orchard said. "What I wanted to look at was what the guarantee is and who's the guarantor of that guarantee and how healthy are they."

Orchard takes an in-depth look at both public and private pensions, the rise of 401(k) retirement plans, Social Security and annuities. The latter is presented in the last half of the film as a means of preserving a guaranteed income stream to guard against an unexpected loss in retirement accounts or reductions to pension or Social Security benefits that may be instituted if those funds become too depleted.

Interspersed with traditional documentary footage and interviews are fictional scenes featuring Abe Mills, an actor and a singer with the band Jericho Road; his wife, Rachel Mills; and their children playing the family of a Florida driving instructor whose plans are muddied when the market drops two months before his planned retirement.

> "I wanted to do a deep dive into pensions, I wanted to do a deep dive into Social Security, I wanted to do a whole deep dive into the deferred comp plans—which is where most people put their money—and then I wanted to do a deep dive into annuities."

Doug Orchard

Experts interviewed for the movie include Nobel Prize-winning economists Robert C. Merton of the Massachusetts Institute of Technology and William F. Sharpe of Stanford University. Other notable names include Olivia S. Mitchell of the Wharton School of the University of Pennsylvania and executive director of the Pension Research Council; Brigitte C. Madrian, dean, Marriott School of Management at Brigham Young University; and David F. Babbel, a Wharton School professor and Goldman Sachs alum.

Government figures include David M. Walker, who served as U.S. comptroller general from 1998 to 2008, a former Social Security trustee and former acting executive director of the Pension Benefit Guaranty Corp.; U.S. Rep. Mike Gallagher, a Republican from Wisconsin who has introduced the Time to Rescue United States' Trusts Act to establish committees tasked with drafting legislation to strengthen federal trust funds on the brink of insolvency; and Eric Cioppa, the 2019 president of the National Association of Insurance Commissioners and Maine insurance commissioner at the time the movie was filmed.

www.ambest.com

Spotlight

It also features industry experts such as Ted Benna, referred to as the "father of the 401(k)"; Edward Siedle, a former Securities and Exchange Commission attorney who pioneered forensic pension audits; Sheryl Moore, chairwoman and founder of Wink Inc., as well as the industry's competitive intelligence expert and fact-checker; and Tom Hegna, host of *Don't Worry, Retire Happy!* on PBS.

The Film's Background

Orchard is a documentarian who has directed seven films including *The Power of Zero*, about the national debt, and *Fasting*, which delves into intermittent fasting as a dietary practice. He said the topic of health has always fascinated him, along with the national debt, which is touched upon in several of his movies.

For *The Baby Boomer Dilemma*, he chose a novel funding technique. Put off by a past attempt at crowdfunding a project through Indiegogo, this time he took a different path. He sold 13 executive producer slots for $15,000 each and contributing producer slots for $10,000 each. To avoid any ties to the backers, real or imagined, he had two other people handle the money and didn't learn the names of donors until the movie was finished, and credits were being made. The film raised about $310,000, he said.

Orchard said the movie was a look in part at what the retirement guarantee is and who is backing that pledge. News accounts of pension deficits in public systems in places such as California and Illinois, as well as looming Social Security deficits, sparked his interest and prompted the movie.

He said the health of those systems was what really interested him. "That's what I felt like would ultimately be most interesting, because that's the part I don't hear anyone talk about," he said. "What happens when it doesn't happen?"

—**Terrence Dopp**

Spotlight

Startup Founder Hopes to Help People Find 'Ferrari in the Garage' by Taking Life Settlements Mainstream

Lucas Siegel, the founder and chief executive officer of Harbor Life Settlements, wants to make the life settlements industry work similarly to the way homes are sold and bought online. By doing that, he's hoping his company and the larger industry will grow by making the process more transparent and navigable for consumers.

At first glance, the real estate market doesn't seem like an obvious comparison to anything touching on the life insurance industry.

Yet the property market is exactly where Lucas Siegel, founder of Harbor Life Settlements, is looking for inspiration as he tries to grow both his company and the life settlements space beyond a niche and into the mainstream.

He's looking toward the "Zillowfication" of a previously opaque world. Such a scenario would include an open market for buying and selling policies—akin to the online real estate portal — that he hopes builds consumer confidence and entices more into the industry. Along the way he wants to make selling insurance policies a go-to component of finance to the benefit of individuals and the larger industry.

"We see the asset class, and the future of this asset class, as something that should be created off a template of real

www.ambest.com

estate," Siegel said. "If you were selling your house, would you sell it to the one guy with a sign that says 'We buy ugly houses'? Or would you put it on MLS [multiple listing service] and try to get a bunch of offers to try and drive up the price?"

Siegel describes Harbor Life Settlements as a marketing technology company operating within the world of life settlements, rather than as an entity focused solely on insurance-related products. He said just 2% of those who would benefit from selling a policy wind up doing so.

"Every year in the U.S. there are some $200 billion in life policies that are lapsing that could have been sold. People just don't know," he said. "That means 98% of the time people are just throwing away their assets that they could have sold."

Overlooked Option

Life settlements involve the sale of life insurance policies for a sum that is above what the carrier would pay out for the cash surrender value but less than the full death benefit. The buyer of the policy must pay all premiums throughout the life of the insured, making life expectancy a critical part of the transactions.

According to a 2021 report by Conning Insurance Research, the life settlements market saw a fifth-straight year of growth in the amount of face value settled in 2020 even amid the disruption caused by the COVID-19 pandemic. The virus could even be a factor in growth going forward, as so-called COVID long-haulers look to settle policies.

The firm's average 10-year forecast of the industry's growth is about $233 billion, and the outlook calls for annual volume of new settlements of $7.3 billion, both figures up from previous estimates. The industry is evolving more toward the direct-to-consumer market, the report said.

To grow it, Siegel is hoping to entice greater consumer interest through My Policy Predictor, an online tool that functions much like the online Zestimate real estate calculators on the website Zillow, which allow homeowners to gauge an approximate value of their home. Based upon that number, they can then decide whether to list the property.

On the professional side, the company also has developed an artificial intelligence tool that combs through the client books of financial advisers and flags those policies ripe for a settlement. Brokers can then notify people of the potential value.

Asset Value

In both cases, if a client thinks the price is attractive enough, they can list the policy through an online auction site on which prospective buyers—hopefully—drive up the price. Harbor Life Settlements bought the underlying code for the exchange from eBay, and the theory is similar in that a consumer will offer the policy and receive bids.

Siegel is betting that increased knowledge on the part of policyholders will translate to a greater comfort and willingness to sell.

"We believe fundamentally that people have the right to know the value of their assets. Period," he said. "They have the right to know the value of their house. They have the right to know the value of their car. And they have the right to know the resale value of their life insurance policy."

The prime benefits are twofold, he said. Expanding the market and making life settlements more common will create an enormous new source of liquidity for Americans, Siegel said. At the same time, he said, every net-worth calculation prepared by advisers based solely on surrender

Spotlight

values is wrong, and the process will become more common through education and transparency.

It's also designed to take an underwriting process that traditionally stretches as much as three months and compress it into a one-minute stage driven by AI.

Siegel said life settlement underwriting has traditionally been painful and inexact; he called estimating life expectancy "brutal." Data-hoarding by carriers has been a long-standing problem, he said.

"They have all the data, but they make money because 90% of people lapse their policy—they pay for 30 years and get nothing," Siegel said. "The less transparent settlements are, the more lapsation will happen, which increases their net worth."

Christopher Conway, a principal and chief development officer at life expectancy underwriter ISC Services, said insurance companies are in the business of taking premiums and managing money rather than paying death benefits. The marketing of life insurance as a needed liability rather than an asset has created a climate in which policyholders too often don't know selling a policy is an option.

"That establishes within the consumer's mind a different perspective about that instrument than it actually possesses or should be applied to it," Conway said. "It creates in the public's mind a perception that this is not the Van Gogh in the basement. It's an obligation and nothing more."

> "We believe fundamentally that people have the right to know the value of their assets. Period. They have the right to know the value of their house. They have the right to know the value of their car. And they have the right to know the resale value of their life insurance policy."
>
> **Lucas Siegel**

Hidden Fees

In 2021, ordinary life insurance lapses fell to a 10-year low of 4.1%, according to *Best's Special Report: US Life: Earnings Decline in 2021 Despite Highest New Premium Growth in Over Three Decades*. To put that number in context, in 2020 there was a total of more than $55.3 trillion of in-force life insurance across the industry.

Yuhmei Chen, a senior financial analyst covering insurance-linked securities at AM Best, said the life settlements industry has gotten more attention since its beginning, with viatical settlements in the early 1980s during the onset of the HIV crisis. In many states, regulations have become more stringent, she said.

Settlements have faced pushback from the life insurance industry because lapse rates are factored into the business models and pricing of most insurance contracts, she said. As a result, some insurance carriers raise the cost of insurance for certain products. Still, Chen said, the lack of transparency has crimped the business.

www.ambest.com

Spotlight

"What people talk about a lot are the hidden fees—the commissions to the broker and the providers' fees," she said. "Brokers are supposed to work for the sellers, the policyholders, to get them the highest price to sell the policy, but from the provider's point of view they want to be able to buy a policy for the least price."

Brokers retain a large amount of control over the process and can factor in those fees, as well as their relationship with prospective buyers, as they present offers to clients. "As a seller you don't really know how many bidders there are because you get the information from the broker. I think that's the thing," Chen said.

John Welcom, who is founder and CEO of Welcome Funds (JW), a life settlements broker in Florida, and chairman of the Life Insurance Settlement Association, said most states have regulations concerning transparency that include upfront disclosure of all fees and a full accounting of the bids JW receives for a policy.

"The fact is that transparency happens on a majority of the transactions that we close," Welcom said. "Every regulated state has a different law, and we have a notice of disclosure within our applications for each state so that we can comply."

Because consumers don't know selling a policy is an option, "it creates in the public's mind a perception that this is not the Van Gogh in the basement. It's an obligation and nothing more."

Christopher Conway

Enough Room

Steven Shapiro, president and chief executive officer at New York-based Q Capital Strategies, a life settlement provider and servicer, said as a buyer he's worked with brokers and also bought policies on Harbor Life's platform. He doesn't see the two as mutually exclusive and said one possible outcome is consumers choosing whichever option makes sense in their case.

Brokers by nature gravitate to larger policies, while technology-focused solutions might be the right choice for people who are looking to sell policies with a smaller face value, he said.

"They're just two different approaches," Shapiro said. "One is using a technology approach to the bidding process, and the other is just using a more personal approach to relationships and calls. I think there's a place for both of them."

Siegel said the technology and Harbor Life Settlements together will change the entire life insurance industry as it inverts the traditional model of how consumers and advisers view settlements. "They've got a Ferrari sitting in the garage that they didn't even realize they had," he said. "It's going to liberate financial advisers to give financial advice."

—Terrence Dopp

Chapter 4: Health

Health Market at a Glance

Health insurers focus principally on providing health care coverage and related protection products. AM Best's database contains annual filing information for more than 1,200 single health insurance companies in the United States.

Health insurers typically have shorter investment horizons than life insurers or property/casualty insurers that focus on liability coverage. Health insurers are measured by premiums and membership in their programs, sometimes known as "covered lives."

The most recent report by the Kaiser Family Foundation estimates that 48.5% of the U.S. population was covered by employer-sponsored health insurance in 2021. Another 21.1% was covered by Medicaid, a joint federal-and-state program for those of limited financial means. Another 14.3% of the population was covered by Medicare, which is designed for seniors. About 8.6% of the U.S. population has no insurance. Individuals who purchase health insurance on their own account for 6.1%, and 1.3% of the population is covered under the military.

Comprehensive health insurance policies pay benefits for insureds for preventative care and when they become ill or injured. Managed care is the most common form of coverage. In managed care, insurance companies establish fee agreements with doctors and hospitals who provide health care services.

If health insurance is provided through employment, the employer typically pays the insurer a set amount of money in advance for all health care costs. The employee may have to contribute a portion of the premium to the employer via a payroll deduction.

www.ambest.com

Chapter 4: Health

US Health – Ownership of Top 10 Urgent Care Centers – 2023 Edition
Ranked by Number of Locations, 2021.

Urgent Care Center/Owner	Locations	% of Total Centers
CVS Minute Clinic/CVS Health	1,246	11.6
Concentra Urgent Care/Select Medical	579	5.4
Healthcare Clinic at Walgreens/Walgreens	486	4.5
AFC Urgent Care/American Family Care	224	2.1
MedExpress Urgent Care/UnitedHealth Group	220	2.1
US Healthworks*/Select Medical	196	1.8
NextCare Urgent Care/NextCare	176	1.6
FastMed Urgent Care/ABRY Partners	134	1.2
The Clinic at Walmart/Walmart	113	1.1
CareNow Urgent Care/HCA Healthcare	110	1.0

*US Healthworks was aquired by Dignity Health in 2015 and subsequently sold to Select Medical in 2018.
Source: Solv Top 100 Urgent Care and Walk-in Clinic Brands.

The employee then pays a flat amount for the services as either a copayment or a percentage of the cost of covered services provided.

In most managed care plans, doctors or hospitals are chosen from a network of providers. Some managed care plans allow visits to doctors outside the network, at a greater cost to the employee.

Some of the largest carriers of health insurance are Blue Cross Blue Shield plans and publicly traded companies. Blue Cross Blue Shield companies operate independently as part of an association. Blue Cross companies originally focused on hospitalization coverage. Blue Shield companies originally focused on coverage for doctor visits. The two associations merged, and its independent licensees now provide health insurance coverage options for employer groups and individuals.

Developing Issues for Health Insurers

Medicaid Enrollment to Decline: The Families First Coronavirus Response Act (FFCRA), enacted early in the pandemic, provided additional federal funding to states as long as eligibility of Medicaid members was maintained for the duration of the COVID-19 public health emergency (PHE). With states unable to conduct eligibility checks and disenroll members through the redetermination process, Medicaid enrollment reached record highs. Some of the new enrollees may have found new employment and transitioned to group commercial coverage but remained enrolled in Medicaid programs due to the inability of states to perform redeterminations. This resulted in much lower utilization and claims costs for the Medicaid segment, leading to record profitability. The Consolidated

Chapter 4: Health

Appropriations Act of 2023 included a provision which no longer ties Medicaid redeterminations to the end of the PHE. States may begin the Medicaid redetermination process and disenroll individuals beginning April 1, 2023. As a result, AM Best expects Medicaid enrollment will begin to moderate in late third quarter 2023, with declines accelerating in the fourth quarter of 2023 and into the first quarter of 2024.

Medicare Advantage Continues to Grow: It is well known that Medicare Advantage (MA) plans have been growing in popularity as these plans offer additional benefits usually at a lower cost compared to traditional Medicare with a Medicare supplement policy. The lower cost of these products combined with additional benefits and budget-conscious seniors has driven a shift in enrollment, with a membership growth rate in the high single digits for the past 10 years. AM Best believes that some of these gains in MA membership have come from traditional Medicare, as an increasing number of members switch during open enrollment. Additionally, the absolute enrollment gains in MA and other health plans has been higher than the increase in total Medicare beneficiaries. According to the Congressional Budget Office Baseline Projections released in May 2022, this trend is expected to continue as the number of individuals in MA steadily rise, and by 2032 MA is expected to have a market penetration rate of 57% compared with over 40% today.

Commercial Market Expected to Be in Focus: The commercial group segment has received less attention from carriers in the recent past, owing to a lack of membership growth, lower regulatory pressures and more-limited opportunities for medical cost management, compared to other lines of business. Large national carriers have focused their attention on the government segment, where continuous revenue growth provides ample opportunities for scaling new technologies and innovative vertical integration.

However, as the group market remains very sizable and ripe for new solutions, several carriers came out with innovative group benefit designs in 2022. Whether these new products will be adopted by the market remains to be seen, but AM Best expects that carriers will increase their focus on offering novel solutions for the group segment.

Dental Insurers Facing Regulatory Pressure: Several states are in the process of implementing minimum loss ratio requirements. In 2022, Massachusetts passed a public ballot measure that requires carriers to meet an annual aggregate loss ratio of 83% for dental plans. If the loss ratio is lower than 83%, the insurer will be required to refund the excess premiums, similar to the minimum medical loss ratio on medical. The New Mexico Office of the Superintendent of Insurance also is implementing a minimum loss ratio requirement for both dental and vision plans. While Massachusetts and New Mexico are finalizing details, other states are contemplating adding a minimum loss ratio requirement with a focus on dental products. Dental earnings could be negatively impacted by minimum loss ratios, which could put more pressure on smaller insurers that tend to have higher expense ratios and lower loss ratios. These companies may not be able to adjust the expense ratio in a short period of time to make the product reasonably profitable.

Mergers & Acquisitions: AM Best expects mergers and acquisitions (M&A) in the segment to be focused on non-insurance operations and vertical integration. Large carriers will continue to look for enhanced capabilities in care management and care delivery, which will allow insurers to lower the cost of care and deliver innovative solutions to clients. Carriers have shown greater interest

Chapter 4: Health

in various types of home health vendors, as well as primary care clinics with multiple locations. These assets remain very fragmented, with many local and regional businesses operating in the market. Large national carriers established a process where the review of various level M&A opportunities is ongoing and only large-scale transactions are discussed publicly.

Major Types of Health Plans

HMO (Health Maintenance Organization): Members select a primary care physician, who oversees all aspects of the member's medical care and provides referrals to specialists. Most services received from doctors or hospitals out of the plan's network are not covered.

PPO (Preferred Provider Organization): A network of doctors, hospitals and other health care providers make up the organization, but the PPO also allows members to see specialists and out-of-network doctors or hospitals without needing prior authorization from a primary care physician. More of the costs to receive care outside the network are shouldered by the member.

POS (Point of Service): The member designates a primary care physician but retains the option to receive services from doctors without a referral or go outside the network for care and shoulder a larger portion of the cost.

Fee-for-service: Also called an indemnity plan, this was once the traditional route for coverage. There is no network of preapproved providers; members can see any doctor or hospital. These plans cost the most and have dwindled sharply in the past 30 years.

High-Deductible Health Plan (HDHP) with a pretax Health Savings Account (HSA): The HSA pays for qualified and routine health care expenses with tax-free money until the deductible is met; then the insurance coverage takes over. HSA funds can be used for expenses the HDHP doesn't cover, and HSA balances carry forward to future years.

Products and Terms

Health products come in a wide variety of forms and address basic health needs, ranging from preventative and basic medical care to specialized forms of illness and accident coverage. Health products include:

Indemnity Health Plan: This may be offered on an individual or group basis. Members choose their own doctor or hospital. The carrier then pays a fixed portion of total charges. Indemnity plans are often known as fee-for-service plans.

High-Deductible Health Plan: This option may feature low premiums and an integrated deductible for both medical and pharmacy costs. Some plans combine a health plan with a Health Savings Account.

Health Savings Account: Participants and/or their employers may contribute pretax money to be used for qualified medical expenses. HSAs, which are portable, must be linked to a high-deductible health insurance policy.

Health Reimbursement Arrangement: An HRA is a fund provided by the employer that employees utilize for covered services. Any leftover funds can carry over from year to year. However, HRAs are not portable.

Chapter 4: Health

Dental Plan: Traditional dental plans may help cover preventive, basic and major services.

Dental Preferred Provider Organization: This plan offers discounts to members who use in-network dental providers.

Vision Plan: A vision care plan may cover regular eye exams, treatment for conditions and assistance with corrective lenses.

Pharmacy: Plans may cover part or all of prescription drug costs.

Flexible Spending Account: A program in which employees may contribute pretax money to be used for medical expenses—including copays, coinsurance and any noncovered services or over-the-counter medication. Funds in a flexible spending account cannot be carried over from year to year.

Medicare Advantage: This provides Medicare-eligible individuals the benefits of traditional Medicare, plus additional features and benefits such as wellness programs and case management services. Individuals who select Medicare Advantage agree to use in-network doctors and hospitals or face much higher out-of-pocket costs.

Common Health Insurance Terms

Coinsurance: For health insurance, it is a percentage of each claim after the deductible is paid by the policyholder. For a 20% health insurance coinsurance clause, the policyholder pays for the deductible plus 20% of covered benefits. After paying 80% of losses up to an out-of-pocket maximum, the insurer starts paying 100% of losses.

Copayment: A predetermined, flat fee an individual pays for covered health care services, in addition to what insurance covers. For example, some HMOs require a $20 copayment for each office visit, regardless of the type or level of services provided during the visit. Copayments are not usually specified by percentages.

Disease Management: A system of coordinated health care services and communications with members who have certain medical conditions.

www.ambest.com

Spotlight

Biometrics Laws and Regulations Poised to Become a Flashpoint for Insurers, Market Watchers Say

The stakes are high for insurers because the penalties faced by their insureds are potentially astronomical.

Biometrics, such as fingerprint readings and retinal scans, have been around for years. But market watchers say their mpact on the insurance industry is just beginning. And in response to recent legal, legislative and regulatory developments, insurers will likely respond with tighter policy wording and deeper risk management, they said.

The first state law to regulate biometric data, the Biometric Information Privacy Act of Illinois, was enacted in 2008 and remains the toughest law of its kind in the country, said Cort Malone with the policyholder firm Anderson Kill. It carries stiff penalties: $1,000 per negligent violation and $5,000 per intentional or reckless violation.

Texas, Washington, Virginia, California, New York and Arkansas all have biometric laws on the books, he said. More laws likely are on the way.

Giving insurers pause is a decision by the Illinois Supreme Court, which in 2021 ruled consumers under BIPA do not have to show they were injured by a violation of the law—just that a violation allegedly occurred.

In *West Bend Mutual Insurance Co. v. Krishna Schaumburg Tan*, the court held a class-action complaint for violations of BIPA—due to the collection and dissemination of customer fingerprints—alleged personal or advertising injury that triggered the insurer's duty to defend, said Andrew Barrios of Reed Smith.

Two important aspects of the ruling should concern insurers and companies using biometric technology, he said.

"First, the court construed the term 'publication' broadly in favor of the insured, defining it to include both communication of information to the public at large and communication of information to a single party," Barrios said in an email. "Second, the court held that the catchall provision of a violation of statutes exclusion did not apply to preclude coverage, construing it narrowly to apply only to statutes governing methods of communication, which the court held did not include BIPA."

The stakes are high for insurers because the penalties faced by their insureds are potentially astronomical. In February 2022 Texas Attorney General Ken Paxton sued Meta, the parent company of Facebook, alleging Meta collected and used Texans' facial geometry data in violation of the Texas Capture or Use of Biometric Identifier Act. Facebook allegedly collected billions of data points that theoretically could generate trillions in penalties, Malone said.

Facebook already was among the tech giants that paid a large amount to settle BIPA complaints, paying $650 million in 2020 to settle one case, records show.

The Illinois law in particular is snaring businesses of all sizes, said Chris Keegan, cyber and technology practice leader at Brown & Brown Insurance.

"We're seeing a really quick uptick in the number of small private actions that are coming in," Keegan said. "They're not the headline cases, but there's a lot of them. They're small, and they add up." BIPA cases in 2020 numbered 264, up from 220 in 2019.

Suits between consumers and companies using—or misusing—biometric devices and data are the first wave, Malone said. "The insurance battles have really just been the tip of the iceberg with the first handful of cases, because one of the things that is happening is that people are letting the underlying biometric litigation play out before gearing up and going into phase two, which is fighting over whether there's going to be coverage for those settlements or not," Malone said. "I do believe the insurance litigation is going to be fairly quick to follow over the next few years."

Along with that, Malone and others said, carriers will tighten up policy wording to broaden exclusions. They'll also dig deeper into company practices and whether they require consent to collect the data, the legal observers said. "They're going to start looking with a jaundiced eye at providing this type of coverage because of the excessive potential penalties out there," Malone said.

The one flip side to that, Malone added, is insurers can do what they've always done—analyze the marketplace, study the risks and come up with premiums that are appropriate for the risks they are being asked to cover.

—Timothy Darragh

Spotlight

Legalized Recreational Marijuana Is a Growing Business With Insurance Challenges

Best's Underwriting Reports and *Best's Loss Control Reports* provide insights into the lines of coverage, exposures and loss control for recreational marijuana dispensaries.

The use of recreational marijuana has been legalized in 19 states and the District of Columbia, with more states considering the possibility, according to the National Organization for the Reform of Marijuana Laws.

But while states with legalization saw sales of cannabis initially rocket to millions of dollars, prices are coming down in areas due to market saturation. Some states are having a hard time getting the legal cannabis industry off the ground, and insurance surrounding recreational marijuana continues to be an issue.

Many large carriers are avoiding insuring state-approved cannabis-related businesses, but for those who do, there are a number of risks and obstacles that need to be considered, according to *Best's Underwriting and Loss Control Resources*.

"Because it is still considered a Schedule 1 drug by the federal government, it's very hard to get bank accounts for these dispensaries, so most of the dispensaries are cash-only businesses," *Best's Underwriting and Loss Control Resources* Senior Assistant Editor Suzanne LaCorte said.

Spotlight

Number of Dispensaries Is Growing

In Michigan, from January to June 2022 the number of growers increased by 71%, and the number of retailers by 17%, according to the *Oakland Press*.

Legal sales of recreational marijuana in New Jersey began in April 2022, according to dispensaries.com. In California, the *Los Angeles Times* writes that "high taxes, local bans and overregulation" are making it difficult for state-licensed vendors to compete with black market dealers.

As the number of recreational marijuana dispensaries has grown, *Best's Underwriting Reports* has identified 10 lines of coverage for the businesses and has ranked the risk exposure associated with the challenges facing the industry.

Those lines are Automobile Liability; General Liability: Premise and Operations; General Liability: Products-Completed Operations; Directors and Officers Liability; Employment Practices Liability; Workers' Compensation; Crime; Property; Business Interruption; and Inland Marine.

Best's Hazard Index ranks the risk exposure for Lines of Business as Low (1-3), Medium (4-6), and High (7-9).

Following are excerpts of the lines of coverage reports that have the highest hazard index rankings.

Best's Hazard Index

Line of Coverage	Best's Hazard Index
Crime	7
General Liability: Premises and Operations	6
General Liability: Products-Completed Operations	6

Lines of Coverage

Crime

The crime exposure for medical marijuana dispensaries will be substantial due to the potential for robberies. Most American dispensaries will only accept cash for purchases because of U.S. federal banking laws that prohibit banks from doing business with companies that cultivate, process or sell marijuana. An employee dishonesty exposure in the form of pilferage of products and embezzlement could also exist.

General Liability: Premises and Operations

The General Liability: Premises and Operations exposure for marijuana dispensaries will be significant due to the potentially large number of daily visitors.

Spotlight

Visitors will include customers, delivery personnel and government inspectors. Slips, trips and falls will be the main exposure. A Cyber Insurance Liability exposure will exist if the dispensary stores customer information on a computer network that can be accessed through the internet.

General Liability: Products-Completed Operations
The General Liability: Products-Completed Operations exposure for marijuana dispensaries will be significant due to the potential for mold, fungus, pesticides and other contaminants in the products, which could make customers sick. Because there are no federal regulations regarding testing the quality of the cannabis products, states have developed their own regulations regarding testing, labeling and packaging. Also, some product labels might not identify the appropriate use or strength of the marijuana, which could result in claims. If the insured bakes or makes marijuana-infused edibles (e.g., brownies, cookies, gummy bears), then this exposure will be increased due to the potential for the food spoiling or for inaccurate dosages in each piece. Because there could be overlap between General Liability: Products-Completed Operations and Professional Liability, both lines of coverage should be written by the same insurer for the same limits if possible.

Loss Control

On-Site Inspection:
- Does the insured have a vault equipped with several tool-, torch-, explosive-, water- and fire-resistant, NRTL-listed, time-delay safes where cash and marijuana are stored?
- Are motion alarms and biometric locks installed throughout the premises?
- Are security cameras placed throughout the premises, including near vaults?
- What is the layout of the premises?
- Are "Employees Only" signs posted outside of all storage areas from which visitors are prohibited, such as where cannabis products are kept?
- Are stockrooms equipped with self-locking doors?
- What types of marijuana does the insured sell?
- Is there a kitchen on site where the insured prepares cookies, candies and other marijuana-infused edibles?
- For edibles, are all ingredients, including nuts, wheat and other allergens, clearly stated on all packages?

—Anthony Bellano

Chapter 5: Reinsurance/Alternative Risk Transfer

Overview of Reinsurance

Broadly put, reinsurance is insurance for insurers.

Insurance companies face many risks in their daily operations, including:
- **Asset risk**, related to the changing nature of investment values.
- **Credit risk**, related to obligations owed by customers and/or debtors.
- **Liability risk**, related to potential losses due to inadequate pricing or reserving, or from catastrophes and other events.

Reinsurance indemnifies the primary insurer against those potential losses. The primary insurer, or ceding company, transfers a portion of risk to the reinsurer. How much risk and what conditions trigger the reinsurance are specified in the treaties. Generally, the primary carrier retains a fair amount of the risk.

Reinsurance allows insurers to increase the maximum amount they can insure. However, most reinsurance contracts do not absolve the ceding insurer of responsibility to pay the insurance claims should the reinsurer fail. The first reinsurance companies were born out of a major fire in 1842 that burned a large section of Hamburg, Germany, and killed at least 50 people. The conflagration exposed the inability of insurers to cope with such a catastrophe, and the insurers recognized the need to distribute risk portfolios among several carriers.

For a basic reinsurance scenario, take an office building worth $20 million. A primary carrier may accept the risk of loss and then turn to a reinsurer, agreeing to cover the first $10 million and ceding the rest. If losses at the building were to exceed the primary layer of

Chapter 5: Reinsurance/Alternative Risk Transfer

$10 million, say $14 million, the reinsurer would be called upon to cover the remaining $4 million.

In a case like this, the arrangement is said to be a nonproportional agreement, also known as an excess of loss agreement. In proportional agreements, the primary insurer and reinsurer share the liability risk proportionately. In the case of a quota share agreement, the primary insurer and reinsurer split the premiums and losses on a fixed percentage basis.

The two basic types of reinsurance arrangements are treaty and facultative. Treaty reinsurance contractually binds the insurer and reinsurer together, with respect to certain specified business. The treaty requires the insurer to cede all the risks specified by the agreement with the reinsurer, and the reinsurer must assume those specified risks. This means that the reinsurer automatically takes the risk for all policies that are covered by the treaty, and not just one particular policy.

Facultative reinsurance, on the other hand, is done more on a case-by-case basis. The reinsurance is issued after an individual analysis of the situation and by deciding coverage case by case. The reinsurer can determine if it wants some or all of the risk associated with that particular policy. This arrangement usually takes place when the risks are so unusual or so large that they aren't covered in the insurance company's standard reinsurance treaties.

Reinsurers also can purchase reinsurance to cover their own risk exposure or to increase their capacity. This process is called a retrocession.

Global Reinsurance – Total Dedicated Reinsurance Capital – 2023 Edition
(US$ Billions)

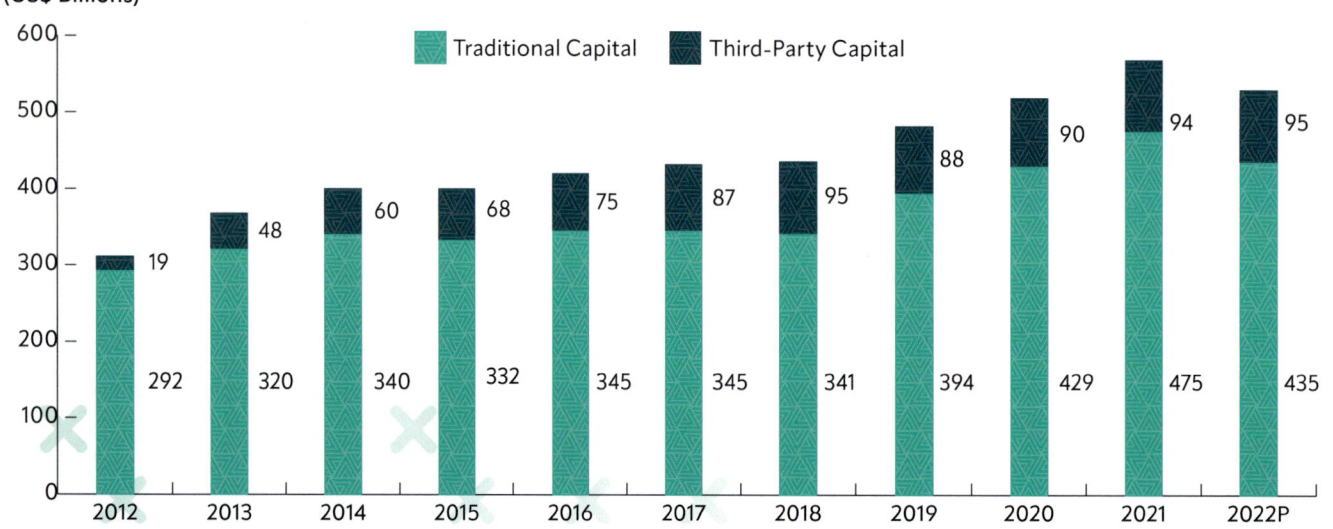

Year	Traditional Capital	Third-Party Capital
2012	292	19
2013	320	48
2014	340	60
2015	332	68
2016	345	75
2017	345	87
2018	341	95
2019	394	88
2020	429	90
2021	475	94
2022P	435	95

Sources: AM Best data and research; Guy Carpenter.

Chapter 5: Reinsurance/Alternative Risk Transfer

Developing Issues in Reinsurance

AM Best's market segment outlook for the global reinsurance industry, issued in late 2022, details issues shaping the environment for reinsurers.

Negative pressures on reinsurers' results over the past few years have been driven not only by traditional natural catastrophe events, but also by the growth of secondary perils, the pandemic and more recently, the Ukraine-Russia conflict. This has been compounded by economic, social and geopolitical uncertainty in general. Although the segment remains well capitalized, the instability of financial results and inability of most players to meet their cost of capital has tested investors' risk tolerance. The accumulation of small to medium-sized events has had a material impact on claims ratios, sometimes at unexpected times of the year (e.g., Winter Storm Uri in Texas) or outside their usual geographical scope (e.g., Hurricane Ida, affecting areas as far north as Canada). Extremely unusual events (such as the weather system Bernd floods in Western Europe) are occurring, as wildfires and floods increase in frequency and severity worldwide.

Some companies have been actively shrinking their property cat exposures or even modifying their organization structures and exiting altogether, although a few players—including some of the largest European reinsurers—seem to see the current environment as an opportunity to improve profit margins and consolidate their market positions even further.

The big question at the moment is about the potential impact that inflation—which remains stubbornly high across the world—may have on ultimate claims.

Global Reinsurance – Primary Insurance vs. Reinsurance NPW Allocations

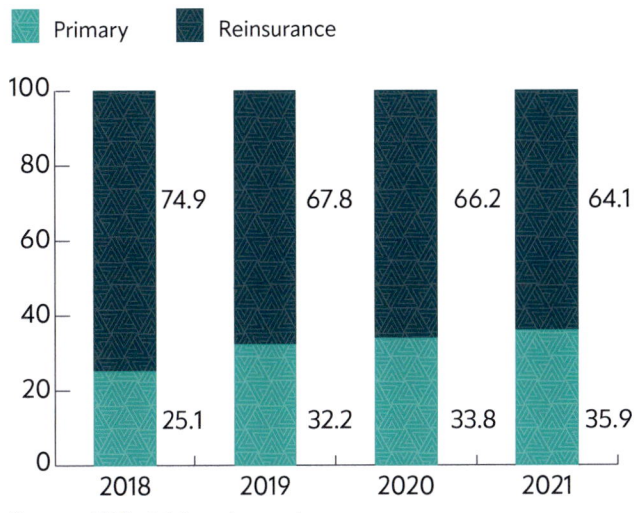

Year	Primary	Reinsurance
2018	25.1	74.9
2019	32.2	67.8
2020	33.8	66.2
2021	35.9	64.1

Sources: AM Best data and research.

A problem that was originally considered temporary (caused mainly by pandemic-related supply chain disruptions) has become more of a long-term concern. This has led, as expected, to steep and ongoing increases in interest rates—with their consequential impact on the stock and credit markets, as well as on economic activity in general.

Unlike previous hardening cycles, new capital has not had a material impact on market conditions. After early signs of enthusiasm and the emergence of a few startups since 2019, execution has been slow and inconsistent. Regulatory and recruitment delays have played a role. Business plans have been downsized or changed suddenly based on opportunistic deals rather than on solid strategies. Several products have not

www.ambest.com

Chapter 5: Reinsurance/Alternative Risk Transfer

yet seen the light of day. Crucially, investors remain extremely cautious.

Third-party capital, while typically expected to react more swiftly to market conditions, seems subject to the same level of skepticism. More restrictive covers, terms and conditions are commonplace. Despite higher demand and improved pricing, the volatility of recent claims remains the key issue. Issues with regard to trapped capital have not gone away completely. "Loss creep" remains well within the memory of investors.

Alternative Risk Transfer and Risk Financing

The blurring of boundaries between insurance and capital markets is most evident in structured finance, part of an area that is broadly known as alternative risk transfer.

The highest-profile members of the ART community are captives—insurance or reinsurance companies owned by their insured clients and located in jurisdictions, or domiciles, that may be tax-friendly or may have reduced capital and reserve requirements. Captives typically are formed by one or more noninsurance companies when traditional market coverage is more limited, or when the parent companies wish to have more direct control of their own risks.

Structured finance is a complex process of transferring risk, often with the purpose of raising capital. Much of the activity revolves around risk securitization, whereby the involved assets are not used as collateral as is typically found in a loan scenario. Instead, funds from investors are advanced to the originator based on the history of those assets, indicating a cash flow into the originator's business. The assets are then transferred by the originator to a separate legal entity—a special purpose vehicle—that in turn issues securities to the investors. Interest and principal paid on those securities are financed by the cash flow.

Insurance-Linked Securities and Structured Transactions

Capital markets participants, reinsurers, brokers and insurers continue to collaborate in various combinations to create new risk-based offerings, including:

Natural Catastrophe Bonds: An alternative to reinsurance, these securities are used by insurers to protect themselves from natural catastrophes. Typically, they pay higher yields because investors could lose their entire stake in the event of a disaster. If the catastrophe happens, the funds go to the insurer to cover claims.

Sidecars: Separate, limited-purpose companies generally formed and funded by investors (usually hedge funds) that work in tandem with insurance companies. The reinsurance sidecar purchases certain insurance policies from an insurer and shares in the profits and risks. It is a way for an insurer to share risk. If the policies have low claim rates while in possession of the sidecar, the investors will make higher returns.

Chapter 5: Reinsurance/Alternative Risk Transfer

Best's Rankings
Top 25 World's Largest Reinsurance Groups – 2023 Edition
Ranked by 2021 Unaffiliated Gross Premiums Written.
(US$ Millions)[1]

Rank	Company Name	Life & Non-Life Gross	Life & Non-Life Net	Non-Life Only Gross	Non-Life Only Net	Total Shareholders' Funds[2]	Loss	Expense	Combined
1	Munich Reinsurance Company	46,836	44,417	32,610	31,482	35,047	68.7	30.9	99.6
2	Swiss Re Ltd.	39,202	36,965	23,131	22,381	23,678	67.4	29.7	97.1
3	Hannover Rück SE[4]	31,443	27,344	21,773	18,827	14,447	69.3	28.7	98
4	Canada Life Re	23,547	23,514	N/A	N/A	23,854	N/A	N/A	N/A
5	SCOR S.E.	19,933	16,242	9,319	7,939	7,251	72	28.6	100.6
6	Berkshire Hathaway Inc.	19,906	19,906	14,285	14,285	514,930	71.9	23.3	95.1
7	Lloyd's[5,6]	19,343	14,263	19,343	14,263	48,242	65.8	29.4	95.2
8	China Reinsurance (Group) Corporation	17,808	16,181	6,956	6,608	16,104	66.6	28.4	95.1
9	Reinsurance Group of America Inc.	13,348	12,513	N/A	N/A	13,014	N/A	N/A	N/A
10	Everest Re Group Ltd.	9,067	8,536	9,067	8,536	10,139	71.6	26.5	98.1
11	PartnerRe Ltd.	8,204	7,134	6,557	5,511	7,544	64.6	25.9	90.5
12	RenaissanceRe Holdings Ltd.	7,834	5,939	7,834	5,939	7,078	74.6	27.5	102.1
13	Korean Reinsurance Company	7,145	5,102	6,043	4,078	2,126	86.4	14.2	100.6
14	Transatlantic Holdings, Inc	6,034	5,387	6,034	5,387	5,398	69.2	30.2	99.5
15	General Insurance Corporation of India[7]	5,821	5,172	5,630	4,987	7,938	88.8	19.3	108.1
16	AXA XL	5,480	4,313	5,480	4,313	13,139	72.6	31.2	103.8
17	Arch Capital Group Ltd.	5,094	3,254	5,094	3,254	13,546	67.8	26.4	94.2
18	MS&AD Insurance Group Holdings, Inc.[7,8,11]	4,393	N/A	4,393	N/A	14,668	N/A	N/A	97.7
19	Pacific LifeCorp	4,098	3,620	N/A	N/A	17,005	N/A	N/A	N/A
20	Sompo International Holdings, Ltd.	3,855	3,417	3,855	3,417	7,433	63.5	29.5	93.1
21	MAPFRE RE, Compañía de Reaseguros S.A.[10]	3,719	3,165	3,080	2,534	2,035	69.3	28.7	98.1
22	Assicurazioni Generali SpA	3,670	3,670	1,242	1,242	36,101	83.5	27.9	111.4
23	R+V Versicherung AG[9]	3,421	3,421	3,421	3,421	2,435	76	26.3	102.2
24	Validus Reinsurance, Ltd.	3,171	2,452	3,171	2,452	3,548	72.4	28.6	101
25	The Toa Reinsurance Company, Limited[7,8]	2,988	2,453	2,127	1,690	2,614	77.6	32.5	110.2

Ratios[3]: Non-Life only.

1. All non-US$ currencies converted to US$ using foreign exchange rate at company's fiscal year-end.
2. As reported on balance sheet, unless otherwise noted.
3. Non-Life only.
4. Net premium written data not reported, net premium earned substituted.
5. Lloyd's premiums are reinsurance only. Premiums for certain groups within the rankings also may include Lloyd's Syndicate premiums when applicable.
6. Total shareholders' funds includes Lloyd's members' assets and Lloyd's central reserves.
7. Fiscal year ended March 31, 2021.
8. Net asset value used for total shareholders' funds.
9. Ratios are as reported and calculated on a gross basis.
10. Premium data excludes intergroup reinsurance.
11. Based on Arch Capital Group Ltd. consolidated financial statements and includes Watford Re segment.

NA = Information not applicable or not available at time of publication.
Sources: AM Best data and research.

Chapter 5: Reinsurance/Alternative Risk Transfer

US Health Premium Ceded by Product – 2023 Edition
($ Billions)

	Affiliated	Non-Affiliated
Medicare Part D	0.6	0
Accident Only/AD&D	0.5	0.3
Critical Illness	0.6	0.2
Limited Benefit	0.1	1
Dental	0.8	0.8
FEHBP	3.5	0
Long-Term Care	2.5	2.2
Medicare Supplement (Medigap)	3.5	1.4
Other Medical	6.3	0.3
LTDI	3.1	4.4
Stop Loss/Excess Loss	4.3	3.2
Medicare Advantage	4.2	3.9
Other Health	5.3	3.6
Comprehensive Major Medical	5.4	6.2
Managed Medicaid	11.6	0.9

Source: BESTLINK, 2022

Surplus Notes and Insurance Trust-Preferred CDOs: Surplus notes and trust-preferred CDOs (collateralized debt obligations) provide another funding source for small and midsized insurance companies that find it costly to issue capital on their own. These companies can access the capital markets through the use of the surplus notes/insurance trust-preferred pools. Securities in these pools are issued by a stand-alone SPV and sold to investors. The proceeds of the notes are used to purchase the transaction's collateral, which consists of surplus notes and insurance trust-preferred securities.

Embedded Value (Closed Block) Securitizations: An insurer can close a block of policies to new business and receive immediate cash from investors in exchange for some or all of the future earnings on that block of business. The pledged assets remain with the insurer and are potentially available in the event of an insolvency.

Securitization of Structured Settlements: A structured settlement is an annuity used for settling personal injury, product liability, medical malpractice and wrongful death cases. The defendant (typically, a liability insurer) discharges its obligation by purchasing an annuity from a highly rated life insurance company. Securitization of annuity cash flows is achieved through the use of a bankruptcy-remote SPV. The issuer of the securities, the SPV, raises funds from investors that are used to purchase annuity cash flows from the annuitants. The cash flows received by the issuer are used primarily to service the principal and interest payments due the investors.

Mortality Catastrophe Bonds: Investors in these bonds lose money only if a level of deaths linked to a catastrophic event exceeds a certain threshold. The event's trigger is extreme (for example, a pandemic). These are a derivative of natural cat bonds.

Life Settlement Securitizations: A life settlement contract is a way for a policyholder to liquidate a life insurance policy. A portfolio of these contracts may be securitized to provide a source of capital. However, certain variables, such as regulatory issues and the uncertainties associated with predicting life expectancies, can create obstacles that may slow their path to the marketplace.

Chapter 5: Reinsurance/Alternative Risk Transfer

Securitization of Reinsurance Recoverables:
Insurance and reinsurance companies have been finding alternative ways to reduce their exposure to uncollectible recoverables and reduce the concentration risk associated with ceded exposures. One approach is the securitization of reinsurance recoverables, which involves a structured debt instrument that transfers risk associated with uncollectible reinsurance to the capital markets. This risk transfer may also be accomplished through the use of collateralized debt obligation technology.

US Reinsurance Ceded – 2023 Edition
($ Thousands)

	Face Amount Ceded	Reinsurance Ceded
2012	24,544,115,924	153,787,611
2013	24,682,585,921	188,836,700
2014	25,334,718,741	98,957,757
2015	25,789,736,121	189,366,383
2016	28,097,632,584	197,264,278
2017	29,381,123,985	220,735,508
2018	32,647,861,345	298,252,008
2019	33,155,639,479	234,907,561
2020	34,941,015,159	295,835,462
2021	35,667,860,746	379,685,905

Source: BESTLINK

Spotlight

FIU Extreme Events Director: Prototype Facility Will Test Forces of a Cat 6 Hurricane

One of the goals of the Florida International University facility is to anticipate and learn from what a Category 6 hurricane would bring. The damage and destruction from a 185 mph sustained event hitting a highly developed U.S. coastline would be unprecedented.

The intensity of hurricanes continues to rise, resulting in higher sustained wind speeds and increased flooding and storm surge. Since 1924 there have been more than three dozen documented hurricanes in the North Atlantic that packed wind speeds of 157 miles per hour or higher and reached a Category 5 level on the Saffir-Simpson Hurricane Wind Scale.

As waters in the Atlantic continue to warm, the potential is created for storms to intensify even more and produce sustained wind speeds that could reach as high as 200 mph. Richard Olson, director of the Extreme Events Institute at Florida International University, spoke with AM Best TV about FIU's grant from the National Science Foundation to design and prototype a facility to test 200 mph winds, waves and storm surge.

"What we're hoping to do is inform the public sector, the private sector and the insurance industry to get ahead of the loss curves, so that the reserves and coverages are tailored for what is coming, not for what has happened in the past."

Following is an edited transcript of the interview.

Spotlight

Can you tell us about the award FIU received from the National Science Foundation and your plans to create a state-of-the-art storm facility that will be able to test the forces of a storm with wind speeds in excess of 200 mph?

The key to understanding what we're facing is to try to stay with and hopefully ahead of nature as nature changes. Hurricanes have three components. They have the wind, of course, which everyone realizes, but there's also the storm surge and the wave action on top of the storm surge. That leads to flooding and water impacts.

People forget that you hide from wind but you run from water. Water is the actual principal cause of death in most hurricanes. Our intention is to design and prototype a facility that can integrate extreme winds, storm surge water movement, wave action and then flooding. You have to get all of the components of a hurricane together in a single experimental facility if we want to truly understand not only what we're facing, but what we will be facing in the years to come.

"Our intention is to design and prototype a facility that can integrate extreme winds, storm surge water movement, wave action and then flooding. You have to get all of the components of a hurricane together in a single experimental facility if we want to truly understand not only what we're facing, but what we will be facing in the years to come."

Richard Olson

How will you partner with other universities and private companies on this project?

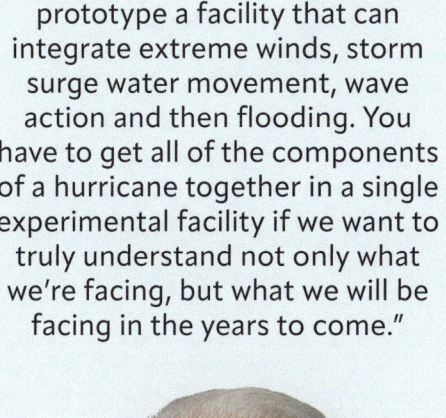

Our university partners, it's a power group. I call it the dream team for research—University of Florida, Oregon State University, Stanford, Notre Dame, Georgia Tech, Illinois, Colorado State, Wayne State and the private firm Aerolab, which has extensive experience with wind tunnel creation.

When you look at the combination of research expertise, it's really important, because this is a complementary team where everybody brings a particular experience and expertise to the table. It's a research dream team, as far as I'm concerned—although our researchers, they're more modest than I am. I can't imagine a better team of research universities.

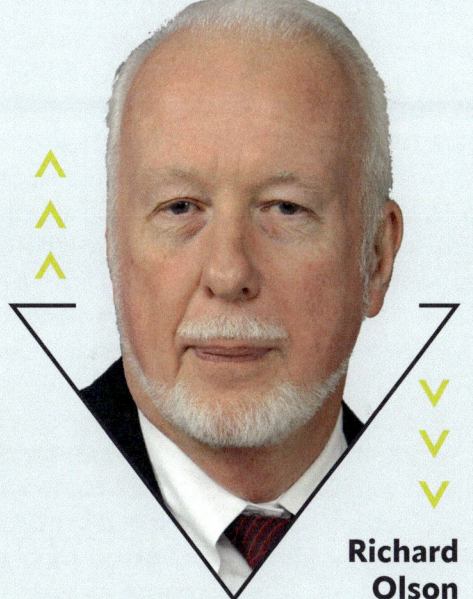

What's driving the rising intensity of hurricanes in the Atlantic Basin, and is that prompting the need for a new category on the Saffir-Simpson scale? What would be the characteristics of a Cat 6 storm and the benefits of such a designation?

First, I have to say that Category 6 does not officially exist for the National Hurricane Center, NOAA's National Hurricane Center. Category 5 starts at 157 mph wind speed.

www.ambest.com

Spotlight

I have to tell you, when I saw Hurricane Patricia off the west coast of Mexico in 2015, Patricia hit 214 mph. Then in 2019, we had Dorian next door to us in the Bahamas. Dorian [winds] hit 185 mph sustained, right next door to South Florida.

Truth of the matter is, Dorian swung at the last minute, thankfully, to the north, but for several days it looked like it was heading up 8th Street in Miami. That really got our attention. This is more personal. When I see a storm at 185 mph or 180 even, anything above that, it just feels like a different—I know I'm not supposed to say that it's a thing, but it felt like a different animal. I was looking at that storm and I was going—I've been through a few hurricanes here—"I am really scared."

It looked different, and I saw those numbers. For us here, we call this our Cat 6 project.

What potential physical damages and other types of losses could a storm of that magnitude cause?

You have your finger on the key question. Dr. Rick Knabb at The Weather Channel, who is a former director of the National Hurricane Center, captured it by saying these storms are bigger, stronger, wetter, slower.

The loss curve, the loss estimates—we have to get ahead of those because right now, it isn't just additive. There are points, obviously, when we're looking at very extreme winds, storm surge and wave action, where we're going to see—or we have the risk of—damage and destruction that we've just never seen before.

You already talked about Dorian and some of the other hurricanes we've seen over the years. In recent years, are there other hurricanes in the Atlantic Basin that would fall into the designation of a Category 6 event?

We've seen what can happen with our urbanization and our coastal development, and the way we get hit, especially within the first 10 to 15 miles of the coastline, by the combinations of wind and water. That includes flooding. None of us will forget Hurricane Katrina in New Orleans and the storm surge along the Gulf Coast.

These are learning events—actually, they're teaching events—but you have to be paying attention to do the learning. For me, Hurricane Dorian in 2019 was a teaching event that we missed, because it didn't hit us, because it swung north.

We didn't actually pay enough attention to what could have happened with a 185 mph sustained storm hitting a major urban area like Miami. We have to get ahead of what storms like Dorian will present to us. It's a challenge to learn from what nature is doing and how nature is changing. The damage and destruction from a 185 mph sustained event hitting a U.S. coastline that is highly developed would be unprecedented.

How will research from the testing facility be used? How will those findings aid in the creation of more-resilient communities and protection of civil infrastructure during extreme events?

One of the keys to what we call community resilience is to see not only the physical components, but how the physical components of resilience will mesh with social, economic and even political aspects. The public wants to be able to trust science and government that we can get ahead of these increasing hazard events.

For me, when you look at resilience, you're looking at it as a multidimensional requirement, and we have to include social, economic, policy, political, public health along with the evolving hazard. It is the challenge of the next 30 to 50 years.

How will insurers be able to use the research and benefit from the findings?
What we're hoping to do is inform the public sector, the private sector and the insurance industry to get ahead of the loss curves so that the reserves and coverages are tailored for what is coming, not for what has happened in the past.

Craig Fugate, the director of FEMA in the Obama administration, had three words to describe resilience. He said insurance is resilience.

No truer words have ever been spoken. The insurance industry is the financial backbone for most people to be able to bounce back, which is vernacular understanding of resilience.

Without the insurance industry, and without [insurers] being, in a sense, together with nature and, from my point of view, ahead of natural hazards, we are going to be in deep trouble. They need to be on the curve—I would say ahead of it—of potential losses.

The losses look like they're going to be going up with these more intense hurricanes.

What are the next steps for the new storm testing facility? When will it be operational? When do you expect to start seeing data and results from the testing?
The National Science Foundation is very careful with its funding. This is a design and prototype project because NSF is not going to invest in a large-scale facility—the eventual facility could be the size of a football stadium. They're not going to do that until we can demonstrate with our university research partners that the design and the prototype at a scale, that they're both feasible. At that point, then the science and the engineering will come together for a major proposal.

Now, time frame. There is a chance that we could retrofit an existing facility and add fans, etc. That's one option. The other option is to build a new facility from the ground up, brand new. We don't know yet. Maybe a retrofit would work. Maybe it would be better to do a facility from the ground up.

Then we will do the prototype, and if everything proves out, then this integration or combination if we go with a different option. Then this kind of research—which would be wind, surge, wave, flooding—I would say in three to four years, we could hopefully be starting that.

Then it's a question of construction. I think we're still looking six, seven years out. We're trying to go as fast as we can, but you can't go too fast or you'll make a mistake.

Spotlight

FIU's Extreme Events Institute has been doing so many exciting things over the years. Can you share some of the other projects you've been working on?
We work very closely with NOAA's National Hurricane Center, which is on the FIU campus. We have been working with them very closely on storm surge in the Caribbean Basin. Not just the islands, but also the east coasts of the Central American nations.

One of the more exciting aspects is that we're providing the technology that supports high-resolution but low-cost storm surge mapping. In many countries, when you get an evacuation order, people don't trust, or have had bad experiences with previous evacuation orders. They don't follow the evacuation. That's what we call life safety risk. We're very enthused about that.

We also have the hurricane public loss model, which is a wind-based model for insurance losses in the state of Florida. One other project that is the basis for what we're doing is the current Wall of Wind, which is a hurricane simulator capable of reaching Category 5, 157 mph. I've seen it hit 162, and it shook me up.

—Lori Chordas

Photo courtesy of NSF-NHERI Wall of Wind, Florida International University

Spotlight

Insurance Leaders: Time to Better Protect, Shore Up Coastal Homeowners' Properties

Insurance leaders say federal, state and local governments need to better protect coastal homeowners from severe weather by making sure their homes are built properly and safeguarded correctly—particularly against floods.

In Louisiana and Texas, the biggest long-term issue is the lack of strong building codes and enforcement of such codes, said Michael Quigley, executive vice president and head of property underwriting & multiline risk quantification, Munich Re U.S.

Jon Schnautz, assistant vice president of state and policy affairs, National Association of Mutual Insurance Companies, said NAMIC has pushed enhanced building codes in many states and "better thought processes into where development occurs in risky areas," as well as tax credits. He also cited inflation as a troubling factor for protecting and rebuilding in coastal states because it impacts the costs of building supplies and repairs.

Schnautz and Quigley both said homeowners insurers can learn from Florida, irrespective of the Sunshine State's problems with fraud.

"The few positives about Florida from a property insurance perspective are the strong building codes and relative quality of the built environment," Quigley said. "All coastal states should focus on strengthening their built environment and increasing community and economic resiliency by promoting mitigation efforts and appropriate land use and by mandating and enforcing stronger building codes that can address the impacts of a changing climate."

www.ambest.com

Spotlight

Insureds won at the federal level in September 2022 when the U.S. House of Representatives passed a stopgap spending bill that includes an extension of the National Flood Insurance Program.

The Biden administration's proposals for reform include ending coverage for properties that see repeated flooding.

AM Best Senior Financial Analyst Anthony Molinaro said that since 5 million Americans nationwide rely on the NFIP each year to protect their homes and businesses, an extension was necessary. "For many of the coastal properties, private insurers cannot compete with the rates offered by NFIP," Molinaro said. "These properties are also considered the most vulnerable. So the long-term solution is still unclear at this point, which is why the U.S. government continues to kick the can down the road every 12 months. But what is clear is that we still need a market to protect these risks, and the NFIP is it right now."

Molinaro said ending coverage for properties that are repeated flood risks would create a protection gap, as homeowners and mortgage holders alike would face availability and affordability issues. "Perhaps one way around this could be for the NFIP to require any properties having repetitive claims to mitigate using some form of federal funding and no-interest loans or sell these properties to the government at fair market value. Unfortunately, some of these properties are in low-income communities where affordability is the issue."

—Anthony Bellano

Chapter 6: Fiscal Fitness & AM Best

Insurance Stands Traditional Product Cycle on Its Head

Most industries work as follows:

- Build product.
- Incur costs.
- Price product.
- Sell product.
- Generate revenue.

But insurance works largely in reverse:

- Build product.
- Price product.
- Sell product.
- Generate revenue.
- Incur costs.

The significance of this reversed revenue/cost cycle is that the product is priced and sold based on an estimate of future costs to be incurred. These estimates can be wrong for any number of reasons, including catastrophes, claim cost inflation, changes in legal climate, newly identified exposures not known at the time the insurance policy was sold, social changes, investment market fluctuations and other factors.

This also means that insurers must be very good at predicting the future and very prudent in administering their business over the long term. This strategy directly results in what are known as underwriting cycles and is why insurance insolvencies sometimes spike in periods following catastrophes or market disruptions.

The insurance industry is less tangible in that the actual cost of its product isn't precisely known at the

Chapter 6: Fiscal Fitness & AM Best

time of sale. The true cost is determined at a later point, often much later. Yet risk is taken on along with unpredictable, exogenous factors that ultimately determine profit or loss. While insurers gauge the probability of a large catastrophic event or some latent liability, these scenarios still cause a supply shock. A simplified explanation is that the insurance cycle is driven by supply and demand. If capacity is lacking, the price of risk transfer goes up.

The Risk of Financial Impairment

The business of insurance, because of the inverted cycle in which revenues are received well before claims are incurred and must be paid (or even known), presents special concerns. There are myriad issues, but the basic concern is assuring to the extent reasonably possible that insurance policy premiums and deposits received by an insurer today will be available for payment of claims and other policy benefits (perhaps many years) in the future.

As a result, the insurance industry is subject to extensive regulation in the United States and in most other countries. In general, regulatory oversight focuses on three primary elements: market soundness, including rate regulation and promoting adequate insurance availability and healthy levels of competition; market conduct, including review of market participant practices to assure proper conduct and fairness in dealings with customers; and financial soundness, including ongoing surveillance of insurance entities' financial condition and a variety of possible regulatory actions that may be taken if there are indications of financial distress.

In the United States, financial soundness regulatory actions may consist of required company action plans, various forms and levels of regulatory supervision and licensure actions. In certain instances these actions are insufficient and the next level of action involves conservation, rehabilitation and/or insolvent liquidation. Conservation is undertaken in certain cases for the purpose of obtaining control of the entity and conserving assets while a review of the situation is conducted. Rehabilitation is undertaken when it appears that special actions are required to maintain the entity's solvency, but with these actions, solvency appears possible. Insolvent liquidation is judged necessary when it is clear that the entity's assets will not be sufficient to discharge all of the entity's obligations.

According to earlier studies by AM Best, impairments varied by line of business, with workers' compensation insurers suffering the most impairments. Fraud has been a frequently identified cause, but most failures can be understood as general business failures associated with poor business strategy/execution and weak management.

State guaranty funds exist to cover unpaid claims of insolvent insurers, but these guaranty funds are generally limited to certain types of insurance and have thresholds of the amounts they can pay. There may also be considerable delays associated with payments by guaranty funds.

It therefore continues to be in the strong interest of policyholders to choose their insurance provider carefully and to monitor the provider's financial health throughout the policy period. AM Best has a strong

Chapter 6: Fiscal Fitness & AM Best

role in this effort by providing interactive ratings evaluations on an ongoing basis.

The AM Best interactive rating process is voluntary and subjects companies to independent, objective evaluations of balance sheet strength, operating performance and other critical factors. Not surprisingly, impairments have occurred much more frequently with companies choosing not to subject themselves to this rigorous process.

Overview: Best's Credit Rating Evaluation

The foundation of AM Best's credit rating process is an ongoing dialogue with the rated company's management. Each interactively rated entity is assigned a rating analyst who manages the interaction with company management and conducts the fundamental credit rating analysis described in AM Best's rating criteria. The analyst monitors the financial and nonfinancial results and significant developments for each rated entity or issue in their portfolio. While ratings are generally updated annually, a rating review can take place any time AM Best becomes aware of a significant development that could impact the rating.

The ongoing monitoring and dialogue with management occurs through scheduled rating meetings, as well as interim discussions on key trends and emerging issues as needed. These meetings afford the rating analyst the opportunity to review factors that may affect the company's rating(s). These factors include its strategic goals, financial objectives and management practices.

Best's Credit Ratings (BCRs) are initially determined and periodically updated through a defined rating committee process. The rating committee itself consists of analytical staff and is chaired by senior rating officers. The committee approach ensures rating consistency across different business segments and

Broad Components of the Rating Process

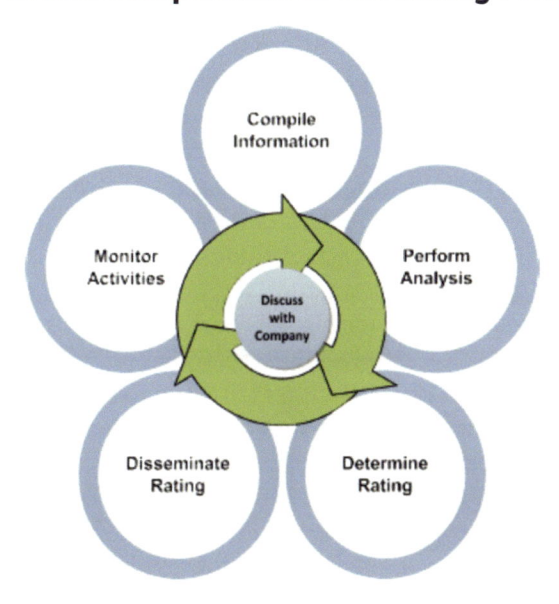

Compile Information — Perform Analysis — Determine Rating — Disseminate Rating — Monitor Activities — Discuss with Company

maintains the integrity of the rating process. The rating process consists of the following:

Compile Information
To develop an initial BCR, or to update an existing BCR, the rating analyst may gather detailed public and proprietary financial information and use this information to develop a tailored agenda for a rating meeting. A scheduled rating meeting with the company is a key source of additional quantitative and qualitative information, including clarification

www.ambest.com

Chapter 6: Fiscal Fitness & AM Best

of information previously received or obtained. Key executives are present to discuss their areas of responsibility, including strategy, distribution, underwriting, reserving, investments, claims, enterprise risk management and overall financial results and projections.

In arriving at a rating decision, AM Best relies primarily on information provided by the rated entity, although other sources of information may be used in the analysis. Typical information provided includes a company's annual and quarterly (if available) financial statements, presented in accordance with the customs or regulatory requirements of the country of domicile. Other information and documents that may be reviewed include, but are not limited to: interim management reports on emerging issues, regulatory filings, certified actuarial and loss reserve reports, investment guidelines, internal capital models, Own Risk and Solvency Assessment reports, annual business plans, Best's Supplemental Rating Questionnaire or other supplemental information requested by AM Best, information provided through scheduled rating meetings and other discussions with management, and information available in the public domain. Ultimately, if AM Best is unable to obtain the information deemed necessary to appropriately review and analyze the rated entity (before or after the initial rating release or subsequent rating update) or if the quality of the information is deemed unsatisfactory, AM Best reserves the right to take a rating action based on reasonable assumptions, withdraw an existing interactive rating, or cease the initiation of any new BCR.

Perform Analysis

The analytical process incorporates a host of quantitative and qualitative measures that evaluate potential risks to an organization's financial health, which can include underwriting, credit, interest rate, country and market risks, as well as economic and regulatory factors. The analysis may include comparisons to peers, industry standards and proprietary benchmarks, as well as the assessment of operating plans, philosophy, management, risk appetite and the implicit or explicit support of a parent or affiliates.

Determine the Rating

All BCRs are initially determined and subsequently updated by a rating committee. The rating analyst prepares a rating recommendation for rating committee review and deliberation based on an analytical process. Each rating recommendation is reviewed and modified, as appropriate, through a rigorous committee process that involves a rating analyst presenting information and findings to committee members. All rating recommendations are voted on and approved by committee. Rating committee members are all rating analysts who have the relevant skills and knowledge to develop the type of rating opinion being discussed.

Best's Long-Term Issuer Credit Rating

Long-Term ICR	FSR
aaa, aa+	A++
aa, aa-	A+
a+, a	A
a-	A-
bbb+, bbb	B++
bbb-	B+
bb+, bb	B
bb-	B-
b+, b	C++
b-	C+
ccc+, ccc	C
ccc-, cc	C-
c	D

ICR = Issuer Credit Rating
FSR = Financial Strength Rating

Note: The rating symbols A++, A+, A, A-, B++, B+ are registered certification marks of AM Best Rating Services Inc.

Chapter 6: Fiscal Fitness & AM Best

Rating opinions reflect a thorough analysis of all information known by AM Best and believed to be relevant to the rating process.

Disseminate the Rating

For BCRs intended to be made public, the rating committee determination is communicated to the entity (or its representatives) being rated before being publicly disseminated. Private BCRs are disseminated directly to the company following the conclusion of the rating committee.

The primary distribution method for the public dissemination of a BCR is the AM Best website; in some cases, it may be republished in a press release. Notification of the rating committee determination to the requesting party serves as the dissemination of a private BCR.

Monitor Activities

Once an interactive BCR is disseminated publicly or privately, AM Best monitors and updates the rating by regularly analyzing the company's creditworthiness. Rating analysts monitor current entity-specific developments (e.g., financial statements, public documents, news events) and trending industry conditions to evaluate their potential impact on ratings. Significant developments can result in an interim rating evaluation, as well as modification of the rating or outlook.

AM Best's Insurance Information Products and Services

About AM Best

Founded in 1899, AM Best is the world's largest credit rating agency specializing in the insurance industry. Headquartered in the United States, the company does business in over 100 countries with regional offices in London, Amsterdam, Dubai, Hong Kong, Singapore and Mexico City.

AM Best Rating Services assesses the creditworthiness of and/or reports on over 16,000 insurance companies worldwide. Our commentary, research and analysis provide additional insight.

AM Best Information Services integrates credit ratings, commentary, research and analysis with insurance news, financial data and thought leadership to help consumers and professionals make informed personal and business decisions.

Below are some of AM Best's wide array of products and services. For more information, visit *www.ambest.com/sales*.

***Best's Insurance Reports*®** is an indispensable resource for understanding the creditworthiness and financial strength of insurance companies. It offers the details and analysis behind Best's Credit Ratings, the latest financial data and company information, along with tools and features to enhance your research.

Best's Financial Suite offers quality, detailed data, insurer ratings and analytical tools for top-tier research. Take advantage of our unique perspective to get a complete picture of the insurance industry. Available data includes:

- Global
- US
- Solvency II
- Canada

www.ambest.com

Chapter 6: Fiscal Fitness & AM Best

Best's Capital Adequacy Ratio Model – P/C, US and Global lets you evaluate an insurer's capitalization and risk profile with a model that is consistent with the methodology used by AM Best analysts, capturing the combined impact of financial risks associated with adverse market conditions.

Best's Aggregates & Averages lets you benchmark insurance company performance against industry aggregates, and observe industry trends.

GUIDE TO BEST'S FINANCIAL STRENGTH RATINGS – (FSR)

A Best's Financial Strength Rating (FSR) is an independent opinion of an insurer's financial strength and ability to meet its ongoing insurance policy and contract obligations. An FSR is not assigned to specific insurance policies or contracts and does not address any other risk, including, but not limited to, an insurer's claims-payment policies or procedures; the ability of the insurer to dispute or deny claims payment on grounds of misrepresentation or fraud; or any specific liability contractually borne by the policy or contract holder. An FSR is not a recommendation to purchase, hold or terminate any insurance policy, contract or any other financial obligation issued by an insurer, nor does it address the suitability of any particular policy or contract for a specific purpose or purchaser. In addition, an FSR may be displayed with a rating identifier, modifier or affiliation code that denotes a unique aspect of the opinion.

Best's Financial Strength Rating (FSR) Scale

Rating Categories	Rating Symbols	Rating Notches*	Category Definitions
Superior	A+	A++	Assigned to insurance companies that have, in our opinion, a superior ability to meet their ongoing insurance obligations.
Excellent	A	A-	Assigned to insurance companies that have, in our opinion, an excellent ability to meet their ongoing insurance obligations.
Good	B+	B++	Assigned to insurance companies that have, in our opinion, a good ability to meet their ongoing insurance obligations.
Fair	B	B-	Assigned to insurance companies that have, in our opinion, a fair ability to meet their ongoing insurance obligations. Financial strength is vulnerable to adverse changes in underwriting and economic conditions.
Marginal	C+	C++	Assigned to insurance companies that have, in our opinion, a marginal ability to meet their ongoing insurance obligations. Financial strength is vulnerable to adverse changes in underwriting and economic conditions.
Weak	C	C-	Assigned to insurance companies that have, in our opinion, a weak ability to meet their ongoing insurance obligations. Financial strength is very vulnerable to adverse changes in underwriting and economic conditions.
Poor	D	-	Assigned to insurance companies that have, in our opinion, a poor ability to meet their ongoing insurance obligations. Financial strength is extremely vulnerable to adverse changes in underwriting and economic conditions.

* Each Best's Financial Strength Rating Category from "A+" to "C" includes a Rating Notch to reflect a gradation of financial strength within the category. A Rating Notch is expressed with either a second plus "+" or a minus "-".

Financial Strength Non-Rating Designations

Designation Symbols	Designation Definitions
E	Status assigned to insurers that are publicly placed, via court order into conservation or rehabilitation, or the international equivalent, or in the absence of a court order, clear regulatory action has been taken to delay or otherwise limit policyholder payments.
F	Status assigned to insurers that are publicly placed via court order into liquidation after a finding of insolvency, or the international equivalent.
S	Status assigned to rated insurance companies to suspend the outstanding FSR when sudden and significant events impact operations and rating implications cannot be evaluated due to a lack of timely or adequate information; or in cases where continued maintenance of the previously published rating opinion is in violation of evolving regulatory requirements.
NR	Status assigned to insurance companies that are not rated; may include previously rated insurance companies or insurance companies that have never been rated by AM Best.

Rating Disclosure – Use and Limitations

A Best's Credit Rating (BCR) is a forward-looking independent and objective opinion regarding an insurer's, issuer's or financial obligation's relative creditworthiness. The opinion represents a comprehensive analysis consisting of a quantitative and qualitative evaluation of balance sheet strength, operating performance, business profile and enterprise risk management or, where appropriate, the specific nature and details of a security. Because a BCR is a forward-looking opinion as of the date it is released, it cannot be considered as a fact or guarantee of future credit quality and therefore cannot be described as accurate or inaccurate. A BCR is a relative measure of risk that implies credit quality and is assigned using a scale with a defined population of categories and notches. Entities or obligations assigned the same BCR symbol developed using the same scale, should not be viewed as completely identical in terms of credit quality. Alternatively, they are alike in category (or notches within a category), but given there is a prescribed progression of categories (and notches) used in assigning the ratings of a much larger population of entities or obligations, the categories (notches) cannot mirror the precise subtleties of risk that are inherent within similarly rated entities or obligations. While a BCR reflects the opinion of A.M. Best Rating Services, Inc. (AM Best) of relative creditworthiness, it is not an indicator or predictor of defined impairment or default probability with respect to any specific insurer, issuer or financial obligation. A BCR is not investment advice, nor should it be construed as a consulting or advisory service, as such; it is not intended to be utilized as a recommendation to purchase, hold or terminate any insurance policy, contract, security or any other financial obligation, nor does it address the suitability of any particular policy or contract for a specific purpose or purchaser. Users of a BCR should not rely on it in making any investment decision; however, if used, the BCR must be considered as only one factor. Users must make their own evaluation of each investment decision. A BCR opinion is provided on an "as is" basis without any expressed or implied warranty. In addition, a BCR may be changed, suspended or withdrawn at any time for any reason at the sole discretion of AM Best.

For the most current version, visit www.ambest.com/ratings/index.html. BCRs are distributed via the AM Best website at *www.ambest.com*. For additional information regarding the development of a BCR and other rating-related information and definitions, including outlooks, modifiers, identifiers and affiliation codes, please refer to the report titled "Guide to Best's Credit Ratings" available at no charge on the AM Best website. BCRs are proprietary and may not be reproduced without permission.

Copyright © 2023 by A.M. Best Company, Inc. and/or its affiliates. ALL RIGHTS RESERVED.   Version 121719

Chapter 6: Fiscal Fitness & AM Best

GUIDE TO BEST'S ISSUER CREDIT RATINGS – (ICR)

A Best's Issuer Credit Rating (ICR) is an independent opinion of an entity's ability to meet its ongoing financial obligations and can be issued on either a long- or short-term basis. A Long-Term ICR is an opinion of an entity's ability to meet its ongoing senior financial obligations, while a Short-Term ICR is an opinion of an entity's ability to meet its ongoing financial obligations with original maturities generally less than one year. An ICR is an opinion regarding the relative future credit risk of an entity. Credit risk is the risk that an entity may not meet its contractual financial obligations as they come due. An ICR does not address any other risk. In addition, an ICR is not a recommendation to buy, sell or hold any securities, contracts or any other financial obligations, nor does it address the suitability of any particular financial obligation for a specific purpose or purchaser. An ICR may be displayed with a rating identifier or modifier that denotes a unique aspect of the opinion.

Best's Long-Term Issuer Credit Rating (Long-Term ICR) Scale

Rating Categories	Rating Symbols	Rating Notches*	Category Definitions
Exceptional	aaa	-	Assigned to entities that have, in our opinion, an exceptional ability to meet their ongoing senior financial obligations.
Superior	aa	aa+ / aa-	Assigned to entities that have, in our opinion, a superior ability to meet their ongoing senior financial obligations.
Excellent	a	a+ / a-	Assigned to entities that have, in our opinion, an excellent ability to meet their ongoing senior financial obligations.
Good	bbb	bbb+ / bbb-	Assigned to entities that have, in our opinion, a good ability to meet their ongoing senior financial obligations.
Fair	bb	bb+ / bb-	Assigned to entities that have, in our opinion, a fair ability to meet their ongoing senior financial obligations. Credit quality is vulnerable to adverse changes in industry and economic conditions.
Marginal	b	b+ / b-	Assigned to entities that have, in our opinion, a marginal ability to meet their ongoing senior financial obligations. Credit quality is vulnerable to adverse changes in industry and economic conditions.
Weak	ccc	ccc+ / ccc-	Assigned to entities that have, in our opinion, a weak ability to meet their ongoing senior financial obligations. Credit quality is vulnerable to adverse changes in industry and economic conditions.
Very Weak	cc	-	Assigned to entities that have, in our opinion, a very weak ability to meet their ongoing senior financial obligations. Credit quality is very vulnerable to adverse changes in industry and economic conditions.
Poor	c	-	Assigned to entities that have, in our opinion, a poor ability to meet their ongoing senior financial obligations. Credit quality is extremely vulnerable to adverse changes in industry and economic conditions.

* Best's Long-Term Issuer Credit Rating Categories from "aa" to "ccc" include Rating Notches to reflect a gradation within the category to indicate whether credit quality is near the top or bottom of a particular Rating Category. Rating Notches are expressed with a "+" (plus) or "-" (minus).

Best's Short-Term Issuer Credit Rating (Short-Term ICR) Scale

Rating Categories	Rating Symbols	Category Definitions
Strongest	AMB-1+	Assigned to entities that have, in our opinion, the strongest ability to repay their short-term financial obligations.
Outstanding	AMB-1	Assigned to entities that have, in our opinion, an outstanding ability to repay their short-term financial obligations.
Satisfactory	AMB-2	Assigned to entities that have, in our opinion, a satisfactory ability to repay their short-term financial obligations.
Adequate	AMB-3	Assigned to entities that have, in our opinion, an adequate ability to repay their short-term financial obligations; however, adverse industry or economic conditions likely will reduce their capacity to meet their financial commitments.
Questionable	AMB-4	Assigned to entities that have, in our opinion, questionable credit quality and are vulnerable to adverse economic or other external changes, which could have a marked impact on their ability to meet their financial commitments.

Long- and Short-Term Issuer Credit Non-Rating Designations

Designation Symbols	Designation Definitions
d	Status assigned to entities (excluding insurers) that are in default or when a bankruptcy petition or similar action has been filed and made public.
e	Status assigned to insurers that are publicly placed, via court order into conservation or rehabilitation, or the international equivalent, or in the absence of a court order, clear regulatory action has been taken to delay or otherwise limit policyholder payments.
f	Status assigned to insurers that are publicly placed via court order into liquidation after a finding of insolvency, or the international equivalent.
s	Status assigned to rated entities to suspend the outstanding ICR when sudden and significant events impact operations and rating implications cannot be evaluated due to a lack of timely or adequate information; or in cases where continued maintenance of the previously published rating opinion is in violation of evolving regulatory requirements.
nr	Status assigned to entities that are not rated; may include previously rated entities or entities that have never been rated by AM Best.

Rating Disclosure: Use and Limitations

A Best's Credit Rating (BCR) is a forward-looking independent and objective opinion regarding an insurer's, issuer's or financial obligation's relative creditworthiness. The opinion represents a comprehensive analysis consisting of a quantitative and qualitative evaluation of balance sheet strength, operating performance, business profile and enterprise risk management or, where appropriate, the specific nature and details of a security. Because a BCR is a forward-looking opinion as of the date it is released, it cannot be considered as a fact or guarantee of future credit quality and therefore cannot be described as accurate or inaccurate. A BCR is a relative measure of risk that implies credit quality and is assigned using a scale with a defined population of categories and notches. Entities or obligations assigned the same BCR symbol developed using the same scale, should not be viewed as completely identical in terms of credit quality. Alternatively, they are alike in category (or notches within a category), but given there is a prescribed progression of categories (and notches) used in assigning the ratings of a much larger population of entities or obligations, the categories (notches) cannot mirror the precise subtleties of risk that are inherent within similarly rated entities or obligations. While a BCR reflects the opinion of A.M. Best Rating Services, Inc. (AM Best) of relative creditworthiness, it is not an indicator or predictor of defined impairment or default probability with respect to any specific insurer, issuer or financial obligation. A BCR is not investment advice, nor should it be construed as a consulting or advisory service, as such; it is not intended to be utilized as a recommendation to purchase, hold or terminate any insurance policy, contract, security or any other financial obligation, nor does it address the suitability of any particular policy or contract for a specific purpose or purchaser. Users of a BCR should not rely on it in making any investment decision; however, if used, the BCR must be considered as only one factor. Users must make their own evaluation of each investment decision. A BCR opinion is provided on an "as is" basis without any expressed or implied warranty. In addition, a BCR may be changed, suspended or withdrawn at any time for any reason at the sole discretion of AM Best.

For the most current version, visit www.ambest.com/ratings/index.html. BCRs are distributed via the AM Best website at *www.ambest.com*. For additional information regarding the development of a BCR and other rating-related information and definitions, including outlooks, modifiers, identifiers and affiliation codes, please refer to the report titled "Guide to Best's Credit Ratings" available at no charge on the AM Best website. BCRs are proprietary and may not be reproduced without permission.

Copyright © 2023 by A.M. Best Company, Inc. and/or its affiliates. ALL RIGHTS RESERVED.   Version 121719

www.ambest.com

Chapter 6: Fiscal Fitness & AM Best

Underwriting & Loss Control Resources presents reports on hundreds of businesses and municipal services, written from the underwriter's and loss control manager's point of view.

Best's News & Research Service provides access to a full spectrum of industry research, analysis and news published by AM Best on the global insurance market.

Other products and services include:

Ratings
- **Best's Credit Ratings - Feed**
- **Best's Credit Ratings Mobile App**
- **Best's Custom Services**

News & Research
- **Best Day**
- **Best's Review**
- **BestWire**
- **Reports, Research and Rankings**
- **Multimedia Resources**

Data Analytics
- **Best's Custom Services**
- **Best's Credit Reports**
- **Best's Financial Reports**
- **Best's Library Center**

Rate Filing Information
- **Best's State Rate Filings®**

Regulatory Filing Application
- **BestESP®**

Additional Services & Programs
- **Advertising Opportunities**
- **Best's Insurance Professional Resources**
- **Best's Preferred Publisher Program**
- **Best's Regulatory Center**
- **Redistribution**
- **Tools to Leverage Your Best's Credit Rating**

To learn more about AM Best products and services, contact our Customer Support Services department via email or at (800) 424-2378 or (908) 439-2200, ext. 5742, 8:30 a.m. to 4:30 p.m. ET.

Spotlight

COVID-19 Mortality Trends, Interest Rates and Climate Change Seen as Key Issues for Actuaries in 2023

Volatility is likely to continue, according to a roundtable discussion at a recent SOA conference.

Actuaries don't typically like uncertainty, but that's what they can expect in 2023, according to Nik Godon, director of insurance consulting and technology at WTW.

Elevated mortality trends, rising interest rates and climate risk were key topics during a roundtable discussion at a recent SOA ImpACT conference in Orlando, Florida. The conference brought together more than 1,600 actuaries to discuss hot topics in the industry and further continuing education.

In addition to its conference, the Society of Actuaries also has launched two new programs: a certificate program for actuaries and others working with data topics involving climate risk, and an affiliate membership supporting the pipeline for new actuaries.

Godon was one of the panelists on "WTW Roundtable—The Circus Is in Town: Rising Interest Rates, Long-Term Impacts of COVID-19 Mortality and More!" Godon spoke with *Best's Review* about these topics, and an edited transcript follows.

The roundtable discussion covered three key topics: interest rates and the economy,

www.ambest.com

Spotlight

COVID-19 mortality, and climate risk. What were some of the takeaways?

I'll start with COVID mortality. In 2020, everyone was asking if the increased mortality was just a blip. It continued in 2022, not necessarily at the same levels as in 2020 and 2021, but still having a material impact on excess deaths in the U.S. The conversation at the roundtable was around the fact that we now know this is likely not just a temporary blip.

There's been an overall increase in the entire U.S. of excess deaths, with COVID being one of the causes. But other causes have also increased recently, such as accidents or overdoses.

So there's this expectation that mortality may be elevated in the near term. A lot of actuaries think there's going to be an extension into 2023 of some kind.

But the broader question is, are there permanent impacts here that might change long-term mortality as a result of COVID? You've had millions of Americans with asymptomatic cases, many of them mild cases, but also many severe cases. And that leaves us with a lot of uncertainty. Is there going to be a permanent impact? And if so, how much?

Should you be assuming some form of increase in mortality, relative to what you thought it might be before COVID?

Some actuaries argue COVID killed off the elderly and those with preexisting conditions, meaning it simply accelerated certain deaths, and maybe the people who are still around are stronger. So maybe mortality will be slightly improved going forward.

There generally seems to be consensus that in the short term you are still going to have some excess mortality happening. But the real debate is over the long term. Are things going to be worse or better? We just don't know. Depending on what actuarial exercise you're doing, some caution or prudence in what you're assuming, with sensitivity testing in either direction, may be the way to go.

> "Part of the roundtable message was volatility is likely going to continue. And from an interest rate perspective, generally people assume: 'Interest rates are up. You guys have been complaining for such a long time that they've been low. Aren't you just super happy?' The answer to that question depends on the blocks of business that you have."

Nik Godon

What about the economic issues?
2022 [was] very volatile, [with] a lot of rapid movement both in inflation and interest rates.

Part of the roundtable message was volatility is likely going to continue. And from an interest rate perspective, generally people assume: "Interest rates are up. You guys have been complaining for such a long time that they've been low. Aren't you just super happy?"

The answer to that question depends on the blocks of business that you have. For longer-term business, like long-term care and universal life, interest rates going up will generally benefit insurance companies longer term. But insurance companies have other blocks like fixed deferred annuities where lots of people have 3% guarantees from older days. A lot of concern had been how long are they going to keep these policies? Now you have this really fast increase in interest rates and people with what were thought to be attractive guarantees of 3% can get a new contract at 5% or more guaranteed for five, seven, 10 years and so on.

Many people think if inflation continues to be high, the Fed will continue to increase interest rates. If we go into recession and inflation gets tamped down, you would expect the Fed to go in the other direction because unemployment's going up and maybe they [increased] interest rates too high.

That goes back to my volatility question. It's hard to know where interest rates may go based on all these other factors, inflation being one of them.

Think of the war on Ukraine. That's part of the driver of increased energy prices and inflation. You've still got supply chain issues. You had all of this pent-up consumption demand from people locked up because of COVID that has been released. That doesn't necessarily go away in the short term either.

A lot of insurance companies over the last few years, as interest rates have been low, have been lengthening the duration of their bonds to protect against further declines in interest rates. And some have been going riskier to compensate for investment yields that have been coming down.

Those things are putting companies, relative to before, in a worse position to benefit from the rise in interest rates. Interest rates going up means the losses on longer-term bonds will have been bigger and you don't have as much money rolling over to take advantage of these higher interest rates.

There's also been spread widening on some of the riskier bonds. So again, if you've gone riskier, you're potentially seeing more of these riskier assets with greater potential losses if you have to sell them. So some actions that companies have taken to try to compensate for lower interest rates could mean they may take more losses and may not be able to benefit as much from the rise in interest rates.

What about climate change?
Climate risk is a core issue for property and casualty companies. They have to worry about storms, fires, floods and the property damage that comes from these natural disasters. It's less obvious how climate risk impacts life insurance actuaries.

There are more demands on insurance companies on the investment side in particular. What is your climate footprint? Are you investing in potential contributors to an increase in climate risk?

There's pressure in disclosing what you are investing in and the climate impact of those investments. You've also got more risk depending on the location of assets. Do you invest in a lot of real estate in Florida?

Another question is what will climate risk, global warming, do from a mortality perspective? If climate risk continues to get worse, there might be some longer-term impacts from both health and mortality perspectives. When there are large heat waves, there typically are excess deaths in the elderly population.

Drought and lack of water is another effect of climate change. Many places are starting to run out of water. What does that mean from a health perspective?

So on the life insurance risk side, it is not fully clear yet how climate is going to impact mortality. There is more short-term focus on the impact on asset and investment.

Should actuaries be concerned about the climate risk issue?

Actuaries should at least start to be aware because their companies are going to have to start disclosing more information on it.

There are new courses and training being developed from an actuarial perspective to provide more insight and background for those who are interested in those topics, such as the climate risk certificate under development by the SOA. Because we do think this topic is going to be growing in importance.

Are there other issues or topics on the minds of actuaries as we head into 2023?

Financial reporting changes for public insurance companies [started] on Jan. 1, 2023. You've got the U.S. GAAP changes known as LDTI—Long Duration Targeted Improvements. If you are an international company, you've got IFRS 17. Some companies have a few more years to deal with the U.S. GAAP changes. If they're privately held, they have at least two more years until 2025. There's a significant amount of effort in the entire industry, not just for actuaries but for accountants, too, to get ready for reporting on what, in some cases, are very significant changes in how insurance business is reported.

There are questions on whether these reporting changes will drive longer-term changes in what products are offered and how we view profitability. That's certainly an ongoing big topic that will continue to be a challenge for people well into 2023 and possibly beyond. So that still is a very hot topic.

M&A is still having a significant impact on the industry. Companies are evaluating whether or not they want to divest of annuity blocks or UL blocks. So that continues to be a hot topic.

Finally, topics around innovation and modernization continue to be at the forefront of industry discussions. The greater use of data in underwriting and ethical considerations surrounding that continue to be an important topic that is growing in importance from an actuarial perspective.

—Patricia Vowinkel

Made in United States
Troutdale, OR
01/05/2024

16712203R00052